To John,

'With our best wishes on your big day'?

Love Noel, Teresa, Daniel & Robin

THE LEGEND OF
JACK CHARLTON

THE LEGEND OF
JACK CHARLTON

TOM HUMPHRIES

Weidenfeld and Nicolson
London

CONTENTS

INTRODUCTION
A KIND OF HOME-COMING
6

CHAPTER ONE
THE FAMILY TRADE
18

CHAPTER TWO
YEARS OF GROWTH
30

CHAPTER THREE
BEYOND THE SIDELINES
46

CHAPTER FOUR
DOGFIGHTS AND DOGMAS
58

CHAPTER FIVE
BACK IN THE USA
78

A KIND OF HOME-COMING

Jack Charlton's gruff personality and frank observations lit up the World Cup terrain like a flare. Press conferences became a sort of Russian roulette, the media squeezing the trigger not knowing what calibre of Charlton mood the barrel was loaded with. Finally, in defeat, Charlton came to say goodbye.

he fourth of July 1994, in the USA: Holland 2 Republic of Ireland 0. DisneyWorld. SeaWorld. Defeatworld. JackieWorld. For a month the best value in Orlando, Florida has been JackieWorld. The only show in town to combine the danger of GatorWorld with the fantasy element of Disney-World. Now on the 4th of July, of all days, the JackieWorld show is closing. The star – Jack, Mr Charlton, Jackie, Sir, Whatever – is leaving town. He's leaving CupWorld.

America seemed an unlikely stage for the son of grimy Northumberland mining country but he has grown into the business as he grows into most things. In this central Florida town where the bor-der between fantasy and reality is a little blurry, where franchised homogenity is the great goal, he has become a cartoon figure made flesh. The walk, when he hurries, has a touch of Groucho about it. The gruff irascibility is a dona-tion from Mr Magoo. The mouth is a sketch artist's hurried squiggle. The hair which has been betraying him brutally since his early twenties flaps comically unless tethered down by a cap or hat. Then there is his size. Put him in any room and he appears to loom above the company like a red-faced lighthouse.

Those of us in HackWorld are going to miss him. Long and loping he has both charmed and terrorised the media at his press conferences. He has made splendid television for the American

Home-coming: Charlton at Dublin airport, July 1994

nation still struggling to grasp the charm of soccer. He has locked horns with FIFA and got lost in airports and sung with the fans and visited Disneyland and raged against the heat and has generally been fine copy for a month.

Monday and defeat. It's going to be a long week for Jack Charlton. In the bowels of the stadium he consoles his players, two of whom have made mistakes which have been instrumental in providing The Netherlands with a ticket to the second round. He makes his way for the final time to the media room.

Outside it's America, or at least the mutated version of America that is Florida during the World Cup. Furious, defiant Irish singing can be heard, every anthem in the thin repertoire of the terrace faithful is getting a good dusting down as defeat is wished away. The Citrus Bowl, a dusty old college gridiron ground trembles with the strange energy and passion of it all. "We love you, Jackie, we do. We love you, Jackie, we do..."

Inside in the cool silence of the media room, for the last time, in this and probably any other World Cup, Jack Charlton begins a press conference. The losing manager gets to speak first while the victor is outside taking the curtain calls, wringing the moment. Jack's last press conference. Who would have thought it. In one incarnation or another he has been at every World Cup since 1966. He looks dog-tired and dangerous. On such days asking him questions is akin to playing Russian roulette. There is silence. Shall we compare Jack to a summer's day? No, he is bruising the media with his baleful stare.

"We lost," he says gruffly, and sucks the life out of his cigar, "and now we are going home."

Home. When it detonates, that little word can cause such devastation. Across the broad Atlantic a nation desperately needed to know if Big Jack Charlton was speaking figuratively or literally when he spoke of home. In that moment, in the wash of a wrenching defeat, home had to be the literal home that it is to those who live in Ireland and to those children of the diaspora who never stop feeling the pull. Home is not a word designed for glib use in Ireland. Home is the old sod, green and damp, forty shades of each. Here in faraway Florida Jack Charlton needs to define his terms. He is talking football while Ireland is talking semiotics. The press conference is brief and without incident. The question of home is all that lingers afterwards.

The meaning of home takes the following two days to unravel. As Irish defeat is digested on either side of the Atlantic the protocol of endings is debated fiercely on talk radio. If Jack was getting appearance money would he be coming "home" asks one caller. The question sends a current through the nation's consciousness. A threshold has been crossed. What a thing to say, what a time to say it. All over Orlando, Irish players, Irish journalists and Irish fans make with the whispers. Did you hear that someone asked Jack if he would be coming home if there was appearance money in it?

The Irish players hang dolefully about the hotel which has penned them in for weeks, most wishing that the incarceration would go on a while longer. A World Cup which started with the giddy defeat of Italy before 60,000 Irish fans in

(Top) Jack in company, World Cup 1994. (Above) JackieWorld – Mr Charlton takes Orlando.

World Cup qualification v Malta, Valetta 1989.

Giants Stadium, New Jersey has ended in the dizzying humidity of Orlando and the singsongs at the bar are half-hearted and dutiful. The complex question of home weighs heavily on the mind.

By Wednesday there has been a sea change. Jack is going home. Old sod home. He pads about the lobby of the graceless Florida vacation hotel making small talk and saying his goodbyes to waiters and waitresses. He's not good at small talk and he's not good at goodbyes. Life in a pit town has left its mark in failing to equip him for life's frills. He's wearing a sheepish smile this morning. The thin line of his mouth droops down like a child's skipping-rope and the great cape of his nose dips gently into the crescent. He is still wearing the cheap straw hat that has been his crowning glory for almost a month now, beneath it his coiled hair lies waiting cobra-like for the chance to spring up.

People mill about the lobby checking in and moving out but Charlton looms above the entire scene, a great outsize caricature of a man around whom the world seems to revolve. There isn't a pair of eyes in the lobby this morning that isn't following Jack Charlton around. Even know-nothing

Jack prior to the Malta game, 1989.

Yanks who have never clapped eyes on him before find him interesting to observe.

The rueful pegged-up smile he is bestowing on all and sundry on this wretchedly humid morning is Jack Charlton's version of waving the white flag. Not a flag he often waves. All week he has been beaten down: by the heat, by opponents, by the authorities, by the media, by the folks back home. The World Cup is over but Jack is still somebody else's possession and he is bristling a little. When it all ended, when Jack and his team finally stepped off the tournament's carousel, the manager's intention was to get on with the business of earning money, honouring his contract to see out the World Cup as an armchair pundit for ITV. Back to the bread and butter.

Across the broad Atlantic, however, an entire

> **Since 1986 Charlton has been the great icon of Irish sport.**

(Top) From the sidelines. Jack directs pre–World Cup 1994 action.

market. In his eight years as Irish manager he has become a marketing phenomenon. Getting Big Jack to announce that he endorses a person/event/product is a lucrative business for Big Jack and the person/event/product. Weeks before Charlton had left for the USA a nationally known politician had got himself into hot water in Ireland for distributing literature outside Lansdowne Road which created the impression that he was personally endorsed in his candidacy for the European elections by Jack Charlton.

The home-coming business sent a *frisson* through this buoyant market which revolves around Jack. The Government of Ireland contacted the Football Association of Ireland, ostensibly to express its concern, privately to implore. Major job losses were occurring in the aeronautical and steel industries at home. Ireland were out of the World Cup. Now this.

Finally Charlton was prevailed upon by officials and PR folk and by his own gut instinct to make the long trek back to Ireland. He would return and take the plaudits of a mixed-up nation and then turn straight around and fly back across the Atlantic again to the bread-and-butter business of punditry. It was a giant concession but by the time Jack made it, the massive stage which was to be the centrepiece of the home-coming had been all but dismantled. Through the night as Charlton flew home 200 minions would struggle to rebuild the structure. All part of Jackie's army as it were. Meanwhile the spontaneity leaked out of the event like air from a punctured wheel.

Thus the final days of Ireland's involvement in USA '94 were a turning point in Jack Charlton's storied relationship with the Irish people and with Irish soccer. Relations didn't get worse, nor did they get better, they simply moved to a different level of complexity, a new level of expectation.

Since 1986 Charlton has been the great icon of Irish sport, his flat Northumbrian manner making a magical but unlikely alchemy with the unpredictable Irish temperament. The history of Irish soccer since the advent of Charlton has essentially been two parallel stories. One story is written in the dry dust of statistics: games played, games won or lost or drawn, tournaments visited.

The other story is slightly more ephemeral, more difficult to get a handle on. That's the tale of a bedraggled island nation on the western outskirts of Europe undergoing mass hypnosis through sport, a community which with a dash of magic realism

nation had sulked like spurned teenagers. Jack Charlton, the nation's sporting totem pole, didn't intend returning to Ireland to be danced around. Win, lose or draw Ireland had promised itself a home-coming party, but in defeat Charlton was playing the hardened old sports professional, decreeing that one win, one draw and two defeats was a record he wasn't much inclined to celebrate. Jack was staying put in the broiling heat of the US of A, thank you very much. No open-top bus ride with the entire Irish cabinet draped conspicuously around his neck this time. No going home.

In Ireland public opinion on the home-coming issue had been mixed but hotly exchanged. The possibility of a backlash against Charlton raised its head briefly. The appearance fee question on radio sent a shiver of panic through the Big Jack

Thinking:
pre–World Cup
days, Malta
1990.

found it was able to suspend real life for the duration of football tournaments. The Irish stumbled upon not just the near hallucinogenic pleasures of top-grade international soccer but a means by which a nation might sentimentalise endlessly about itself, might look at itself in the looking-glass that a great televised event provides and decide that it likes what it sees. Aren't we the greatest fans in the world? Have you ever met any race who can drink as much as us? And still be so friendly? I'm tellin' ya, buddy, we're a great little nation.

There was, too, a third strand to the narrative, one which linked both stories – Jack Charlton's own growth. In the hierarchy of needs, his long glorious career with Leeds United and England had provided Charlton with almost everything: security, comradeship, esteem, ego, everything but self-actualisation. Back in 1986 when he was still a splintery Englishman uncommonly confident in the weight of his own wisdom he would never have made this gracious concession to travel to Ireland merely to satisfy the whim of the people. No, not the hard-talking curmudgeon who invited a journalist outside to settle an argument

Man and Ball in Malta, 1990.

with fists at his very first press conference as Irish manager. Now his intuition about loyalty and people was propelling him eastwards across the Atlantic. "It's the right thing to do," he said.

As it transpired, coming home was indeed the right thing to do. In the wake of the World Cup exit, for the first time, the stories had failed to run in parallel lines. The plot was all over the place. Charlton in defeat saw nothing to celebrate. While Ireland and its millions of emigrants scattered like seed throughout the world had been in a state of delirium for three weeks, Charlton hadn't enjoyed the World Cup. The tournament had been about pressure and hassle and controversy and heat. He pined for the company of his grandchildren,

longed for the tranquillity of a river bank. Ireland, meanwhile – at least a strident and vocal part of Ireland – demanded celebration regardless of results. Jack Charlton appeared to be yards offside.

He has spoken often about his native England and how history has distorted English sporting expectations. Mere participation is never sufficient for the English but it is traditionally a source of joy for the Irish. Through its honesty and zest Charlton's team had hitherto precisely matched the internal expectations of the Irish people and of Charlton himself. However, in the heat of Florida, playing with a new and initially promising tactical formation, players had wilted and something had gone askew in the relationship between

the people and Jack Charlton. The road to fulfilment seemed to have reached a parting.

Moral victories like participation and the avoidance of humiliation or mass arrests were no longer sufficient unto the day. After the opening game with Italy, the first time Ireland had actually won a match in two World Cups, expectations changed. The shoulder-shrugging "you draw some, you lose some" philosophy was gone for ever. Whoever designed the points system for soccer had been right all along. Winning was better than drawing. Hardened professionals appreciated that fact always. The rest of Ireland hadn't previously developed football thought far enough, however. Qualifying was better than not qualifying; drawing was better than losing. Those were the corner-stones of a nation's happy philosophy prior to the defeat of Italy. When post-Italy, the team lost two and drew one of their next three games some reflex of the heart still wanted the jigs and the reels and the whole feel-good package. The newfangled winning business was all very well but qualifying was still better than not qualifying, wasn't it. Are you watching, Enger-land?

The Irish desire to perform the hokey-pokey and shake it all about, even in the hour of defeat, is borne of a self-consciousness to which Jack Charlton through breeding and background is unavoidably alien. Over eight years and through three major soccer tournaments a great and occasionally stifling national hubris has derived from the bald fact that Irish soccer supporters decline to rape and pillage foreign towns as soccer stereotypicality demands. Always looking on the bright side of life has become the national sporting trademark retailed enthusiastically across the football stadiums of the earth.

Irish soccer fans, or "the greatest supporters in the world" as the battalions who have formed behind Charlton are traditionally known, have become a tale unto themselves. At least four books have been spawned on the phenomenon. Irish newspapers send separate reporters to cover the fans' story every time the soccer team ventures abroad.

Sports Illustrated, the leading

Mmmmmmm – the national anthem is in bloody Gaelic.

American sports magazine, felt compelled to devote a large feature article to the Irish-fan phenomenon during the US World Cup. As Irish supporters tirelessly compared themselves favourably with the subhuman species who trail after the English soccer team, reporter Alexander Wolff had the key difference between the tribes explained to him. "In Ireland," said a proud fan, "how to drink is something that is bred into us."

With a few honourable exceptions, English newspaper writers have presented a distorted and somewhat patronising view of the entire Charlton era. The composite introduction to a Charlton piece will always mention the parties and the popularity of Big Jack, which exceeds that of the Pope. They will note cleverly that Irish eyes are smiling. Typically Big Jack's Jolly Green Army will roll into a town somewhere surfing on a tidal wave of Guinness and song and waving their shillelaghs at the auld enemy. Their prayers might be answered, they might not. Either way they will have a party.

In reality we haven't so much been waving as drowning. In defeat, even a defeat as prosaic and

Charlton and his players have developed a strange and perhaps unbreakable bond with the Irish public.

negligent as that against the Dutch in Florida which ended Ireland's World Cup adventure, the national wonder of the greatest, most luminous fans in the world, the fans who pluckily always ferreted out the bright side of life, the fans who were taken from their classrooms at the age of six to remote camps to be trained in drinking technique, none of that could be allowed to die. Ordinary life was too grim to go back to.

Jack Charlton couldn't profess to understand this remorseless need for celebration and communion but grasped his own role in its perpetuation and recognised the innate decency of the individuals behind the songs and the scarves. He and his players have developed a strange and perhaps unbreakable bond with the Irish public, a symbi-

otic relationship that provides the team with wind for its sails and the nation with a prism through which to define itself positively without the distorting effects of hard times and a war that rattles on eternally across the jagged seam that divides the country.

For eight years the manager and his team have provided the excuse for a great cultural fantasy, the pretext for a wonderful piece of mass escapism. Over the entire pageant Jack Charlton has floated along rising and falling like a kite on the winds of excitement and affection. Jack Charlton, the legend of Leeds United and England, the quintessential Englishman enjoying an unlikely Indian summer's worth of glory in a neighbouring territory. Loved and revered as he had never been at home. As

Supermodel

another World Cup ended, however, the thread seemed to be fraying. The wars had been merry as usual but afterwards the songs seemed a little sadder. Jack Charlton noted the waning innocence among the disciples but bowed to their expressed desire that he return to Ireland.

So on this Wednesday morning he is heading for home, or the great ersatz version of home that is his existence on Irish soil. With his players around him he ambles out into the Florida heat and climbs the steps of the team coach. There is an end-of-era feel to the moment. His players are a mix of the old and the promising. This particular group will never inhabit a dressing room again, will never make another journey together after this one.

Orlando to Dublin via New York is a long haul for a man who has endured six weeks of constant pressure and who must make the return journey within twelve hours of touchdown. As flight EI 108 made the interminable slog over the Atlantic, through night and on to morning, Charlton paced the aisles impatient and grumpy, signing autographs but declining to chat or linger. Eventually he settled down to a shallow sleep and waited for Ireland to engulf him upon waking.

Thursday morning and Ireland presented itself in cliché form for the final twenty minutes of the flight home. Nothing but early morning blue skies above, nothing but ragged green fields and gentle knolls speeding past below. The pull of home was palpable. The breath of Ireland filled the cabin and lifted the spirits.

On the runway when at last the door of the white 747 was peeled back and the long string of unvarnished Northumbrian football stock presented himself to the assembled multitudes the response was not the wide-eyed delirium and hysteria which characterised previous home-comings on this same runway. What permeated the morning air was a sense of gratitude, a massive silent thank you, rolling in waves towards Charlton, for eight years of distraction and pleasure and heartbreak and fond foolishness, much thanks.

The fleeting visit was enough to retune Charlton's intuition. In the weeks that followed he would speak of the need to change the Irish way of playing, the need to move beyond the gallant underdog image which had served the nation so durably. Fulfilment through soccer would have a different, more complex expression in the future.

By returning home Jack Charlton had kept the beautiful spell alive, had kept the stories progress-

ing along parallel lines. If there was despondency it would be shared, if there was to be a wake he had come home for it. Times ahead would be different, surely, but for the moment he was emerging from the shiny aircraft and heading away to hear the roars of thousands in Phoenix Park. It wasn't spontaneous, it was a little stilted, a little formal, a tad contrived, but the confusion had been banished. His very presence was proof of a mutual affection which went deeper than mere gratitude for some good soccer results.

On the top of the steps, stooping as he came through the aircraft door, Charlton's famous face crumpled into a corrugated grin. The right hand described a perfect arc as it acknowledged the immense blast of human warmth. The favourite son was home, his relationship with Ireland growing ever more complex. The legend of Jack Charlton growing ever greater.

(Top) Some kind of home-coming. Preparations underway for Ireland's return from US 1994. (Above) 'We love you Jackie, we do' – Irish fans in Phoenix Park, July 1994.

CHAPTER ONE

THE FAMILY TRADE

For Jack Charlton football was always the family profession, passed on through the generations. Some sense of loyalty to his home-place sent him down the pits at Ashington, but football and Leeds United lured him from a lifetime's grind. Today he is the last practitioner of the old family trade.

To unravel Jack Charlton, first you have to unravel the bloodlines. For as long as soccer has been played for money the Charltons or the Milburns have drawn a wage from the game. Well over a century onwards and the last of the line, the last to indulge in the family madness is Jack Charlton. Prosperity has driven the clan away from the playing pitches. Jack and Bobby Charlton, brothers and fourth-generation footballers, took the family as far as it could travel when they both won World Cup medals on a fabled day at Wembley in 1966. Bobby makes his living in boardrooms and business halls now. Only Jack still wears the studs, still tramples the grass.

The Ashington of his childhood was a gaunt working town whose male young provided fodder for the mines or recruits for the great footballing empires of Sunderland and Newcastle. The charismatic pull of those two clubs was sufficient for Ashington's own team to be forced to abandon its attempts to sustain itself in the Northern section of the English league. From the shipyards to the coal seams Newcastle and Sunderland drew their fanatical support.

When Newcastle ended a long famine by winning the FA Cup at Wembley in 1951 some half a million people welcomed them back to their home town. Half a million people was almost twice the city's population. The mining towns had emptied out in homage. Jackie Milburn scored two Wembley goals against Blackpool that weekend, the second of which, a twenty-yard drive, is etched on the folk memory of the north-east. The town called the big striding centre-forward Wor Jackie Milburn. The Charlton boys just called him Uncle Jack.

From football there were thrills to be had and lessons to be learned. Lessons about life and competing and honesty and effort and about the

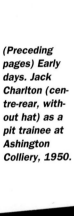 

(Preceding pages) Early days. Jack Charlton (centre-rear, without hat) as a pit trainee at Ashington Colliery, 1950.

value of a few shillings. A famous story of the era concerns Sunderland's purchase of the legendary Len Shackleton from Newcastle. Guessing that Bolton Wanderers would offer Newcastle an even £20,000 for Shackleton's services, the Sunderland chairman Colonel Joe Prior offered Newcastle £20,050. A horse dealer's bid. Newcastle allowed Shackleton to depart to their great local rivals in return for the extra fifty pounds.

Between the wars poverty had scarred the community in much the way that mining scarred the landscape. Death underground was a frequent occurrence and fatherless families turned in on the community for help and the community turned in on itself facing away from the world in the struggle for survival. Football existed as the people's only opiate and they indulged enthusiastically and with a fervour that Jack Charlton often glimpses again some fifty years later in another era in another country. Football was a cultural expression.

There are moments in modern Ireland when the country seems to be failing on every level that matters. "Sure, isn't the country banjaxed," says Gay Byrne, the voice of middle-class Ireland on his morning radio show. The nation seems to endure such a steady hail of misfortunes that only the abstract fails to get washed away. History lessons linger hazily in the race memory. The remnants of a once great culture are turned to commercial use. To survive is to be able to just keep on keeping on. The weight of despair pins the country down and makes the reservoir of national self-confidence a shallow resource. The country is left grasping a brittle rudimentary form of defiant nationalism which bubbles up in times of trouble, in times of intoxication and in response to traditional stimuli. Soccer and Jack Charlton's team have provided a means of exploring that phenomenon. In the drizzle of Lansdowne Road the chant builds up slowly, "You'll never beat the Irish, you'll never beat the Irish, you'll never beat the Irish." It's a stirring thought but unsustainable in the real world on the other side of the turnstile.

In extremis so it was with north-eastern England in the days of Jack Charlton's youth and before. Pit towns have always been self-sufficient and hard but Durham and Northumberland amounted almost to an autonomous state. Between the wars they bore the bad times with stoic heroism until they could take no more and eventually in one of the century's most poignant gestures of mass despair they

A 12-year-old Jackie, 1947.

seeped out in a great river of humanity from Jarrow and around to march to London. Think of Liverpool in the seventies and the eighties, a great city being slowly raped and turned over, and picture the fanaticism that breathed life into Everton FC and Liverpool FC. So it is with Ireland and Jack Charlton's team, so it was with north-east England. Soccer is a valve for the bad times.

In the Northumbrian summer, boys would tramp to school in their bare feet to save the leather for the winter and for football. The local headmaster Stuart Hemingway witnessed the cruellest times between the wars when hunger cut into the very flesh of the community. Hemingway came to regard football as a tool of working-class emancipation, a tool as valuable as learning. As a

young teacher he had viewed the game disapprovingly, dismissing it as escapism, but through the bad years Hemingway came to realise that football might be escapism but it was escape too. "I came to think that this professional football was nothing bad at all. That this chasing after schoolboys by professional clubs was a good thing. Four pounds was the young footballer's weekly wage at the time. More than the pits gave a man." The region duly gave up stars as readily as it gave up its black mineral riches: Raich Carter, Wor Jackie, Colin Veitch, Jack Hill, George Camsell, Wilf Mannion, Len Shackleton and many, many more preceded the Charltons.

The cheek-by-jowl neighbouring counties of Northumberland and Durham boasted some 1300

Early signs. Jack (middle row, far right) with the Hirst Park Modern School football team, 1949.

minor and junior sides by the fifties and the area was regarded as the nursery of English football. At one stage in the late forties, twenty managers of English or Scottish clubs came from either Durham or Northumberland, Tom Whitaker of mighty Arsenal being the most famous of them all. One junior club, Birtley had eighty former players making their living in the league at one time. Clubs from all over England ran summer coaching schools in the north-east and those with serious ambition stationed permanent scouts there. It was said that a lad couldn't idly kick a pebble on the way to school without a scout noting which was the favoured foot.

So if the Charlton boys scuffling until nightfall over a rag ball on Beatrice Street already had the family trade of soccer to buffer them against the worst of Northumberland's lean years they had, too, Stuart Hemingway looking out for the footballing interests of both Jack and Bobby (although he taught only the former) and the soccer clubs of the country raking the area for talent. The footballing vocation always beckoned.

The family trade, the vocation. Tracing back through the bloodlines Jack's mother Cissie is the pivot, the matriarch and the link between the Milburns and the Charltons. Cissie was a wondrous dribbler of the ball herself, a sight to behold outside the narrow terraced line of houses that formed Beatrice Street. When her second son Bobby, our kid, announced himself early as a childhood prodigy Cissie would push him along, marking out pitches of a summer evening upon which to coach him and coax him. She would pace out the sprints, twenty yards then jog back again, eighty yards then jog back again. Now do it dribbling the ball. Now some shooting. So it went.

Her eldest, the gangly roguish Jack was a more solitary figure whose pleasure in life was to wander alone through the hedgerows and ditches of the Northumberland countryside. Those lonesome expeditions have defined the man far more indelibly than Cissie's coaching defined Bobby. In manhood it is Jack who retains the closest ties to home and to the land, Jack who traces his finger through the family tree with such wonder. It was

Newcastle United, 1951, with Jackie Milburn (front row, second from right)

Family get
together,
c. 1954. Jack
and Bobby (far
right) with
their parents
Cissie and Bob
(third and
fourth from
right), with the
Milburns (from
left) – George,
Jack, Jimmy,
Wor Jackie and
Stan).

Jack who when the money rolled in during the sixties installed his mother in the new house which she christened Jules Rimet and which still bears that name although the premises have since changed hands. Jack likes the land, he likes the heritage and most of all perhaps he savours the history.

Tanner Milburn, or "Tannah Milburn" as Jack pronounces the name, was a goalkeeper of some note and Cissie's father. Tanner's father before him was a professional of considerable longevity and standing in the north-east. "The old war-horse they called him," says Jack proudly.

And Cissie was of course what Jack calls a "full cousin" of the north-eastern footballing legend Jackie Milburn. "Wor Jackie Milburn," Charlton will say these days, "you've heard of him, surely." Cissie's four brothers all plied the family trade too. Each was a full-back. The defending, hard-tackling Milburn boys: Jackie, Jimmy, George and Stan.

Mining was also in the family. Cissie's husband

> **Cissie was a what Jack calls a "full cousin" of Jackie Milburn.**

Bob spent his days in the netherworld at the bottom of a shaft. In Ashington and the towns around it in those days when men would talk to each other on the streets, as they made conversation and passed the time, they would stoop, one hand wandering around to console the aching lower back. That was the working pose from fifteen years of age onwards. Bent and stooped as they worked the seam in the tunnel twelve hours a day, bent and stooped and wheezing.

Football and mining. The Charlton boys were fortunate in that two vistas opened before them. Twice as many as beckoned most of the children they played with. Cissie and Bob had four sons. Two pairs really, Jack and Bobby, Gordon and Tommy. Between Jack's arrival and Bobby's birth there lay twenty-eight months. Close enough for them to be confederates. Jack can scarcely remember a time when he and Bobby didn't kick a football of some description around together, his small brother frustrating him with the sorcery that would become his hallmark, Jack developing the doggedness that would become his.

They were bathed early in the waters that would mark them as followers of the football faith. Cissie would push Jack and Bobby in a pram to any town in the vicinity where Ashington happened to be playing. When the roar of the crowd

Jack with his 16-year-old brother Gordon, who had just signed with Leeds, 1959.

would greet a goal the two toddlers would start and stir in their pram with shock and excitement. As they grew into an early form of spiky independence Jack and Bobby would be permitted to make their own pilgrimages. They'd go to Blythe or Whitley Bay or beyond to see the local boys play, Jackie always entrusted with the task of watching out for Bobby. On occasion they'd be placed on a bus to Newcastle and Wor Jackie Milburn would install them safely in St James Park that they might watch the professional wonders of Newcastle United perform.

It was Bobby, though, who burst with potential. The older brother lived in the younger's shadows. Jack played for the local YMCA Under

18 side when he was just fifteen but the star of that team was twelve-year-old Bobby. For decades that would be the pattern; Bobby's swerves and shots and solidity outshining his brother's stringy determination and pit-town savvy. Jack recalls the YMCA side struggling around their young star, trudging home on winter Saturdays on the mean end of seventeen or eighteen goal hidings. Glamour? They drew two apiece with Blackhole once and talked about it till the season ended. The first football jerseys they wore in school were maroon and heavy. The curtains they had been cut from were maroon and heavy too, a relic of the blackouts.

Charlton's childhood was about engrossed

knots of schoolboys hacking a football about in cinder yards but it was also about long forays off on his own wandering the fields and rivers and forests of the open country. To the north and north-west of Ashington was the land and to the east was the sea. Below was the grimy industrial sprawl that began at Newcastle and stretched ever southwards, towns which earned his familiarity but never his trust.

"I knew the towns," Jack Charlton says, "but the country was my place. Miles you could go without meeting a soul and yet just to the south were crowded towns."

Young Jack taught himself to fish, painstakingly by trial and error and stolen glances at his elders, experimenting contentedly with flies and lines until he evolved a unique expertise. He went bird-nesting and his father added to his education by sharing the secrets of the hunt, how to work a whippet or a lurcher, how to snare rabbits and trap ferrets and track animals. He learnt the habits of nature and the tricks of tides and the songs of the birds.

Some distillation of the north-east seeped into Jack in a manner that bypassed Bobby.

Some distillation of the north-east seeped into Jack Charlton then in a manner that bypassed Bobby. He lives there still and loves the long drives north of his home when he might travel for an hour without meeting another car, when he might upon a whim open the boot and jig a fly to a line and stand upon the bank at peace waiting for a pull. He mourns the passing of the community he loved, its destruction during the crazed deindustrialising rape of the Thatcherite eighties. Television is rendering the world homogenous. "Nobody talks Geordie any more," he says, then corrects himself in the vernacular, "I mean, nobody tekks Geordie."

By reflex of conviction in the eighties he lent his support to the miners' strike, sharing his voice and his money and his influence with the community he sprang from, a community that has never had to ask questions about Jack Charlton's loyalty. The rugged country, the dark querulous sea and the long ruler-straight terraces of houses all shaped him. When schooldays were over, some undefinable sense of place led him to don the

boots of the pit rather than the pitch. It's often said about Charlton that when it comes to contrariness he is a world-class performer. Opting to join the ranks of the bent, broken and wheezing men of Ashington scraping away at the innards of the earth instead of setting out immediately to make his mark in the glory game can only copper-fasten that reputation or mark him as a man whose foundations are a deep-rooted sense of home place and common decency.

"I had to see what the mines were like," he says, as if it were the most obvious thing in the world. "Me father worked there all his life. I had to know about it." He isn't a man to offer up romanticised versions of his past, however. Not about the pits which inhaled and exhaled the community he loved for decades before finally coughing them up one last time.

He trained for sixteen weeks, through college and practical pit work, enjoying the variety and winding up "on the bank" or above the ground in a weigh room with a friend called Jackie Somers. Pleasant days. The wagons trundled in, were weighed and ticketed while the banter above continued unabated and then trundled out again to their dark destination below the earth. He might have stuck with it, too, but for the fact that when they deemed him good enough and ready enough they moved him to his father's pit at Linton and unveiled the rest of his life for him. To this day he becomes animated when he describes the scene. "Hanging on and knocking off it was called. That was my job, hanging on and knocking off. Forty-

A different ball game. Jack and Bobby, at Newcastle's cricket ground, enjoy their celebrity status after the 1966 World Cup victory.

three years later I can picture the scene, I can tell you exactly where everything was."

Tubs would arrive from the bowels of the pit on a haulage wire and would pass over the "hanger-on and knocker-offer's" head. So long as the haulage wire moved and the tubs were properly latched on everything was fluid. The job entailed using a long lever called a handboden to take the pressure of weight off sufficiently for the full tubs to be knocked off and emptied. The line had to be kept moving at all times. Flying tubs were to be avoided. When the wire was pulled down in order to empty a tub the line and tub would both snap suddenly back up into the air when the task was done and the operative had to jump back quickly. In the case of emergency there was a bell in the corner which could be rung. Nobody wanted to hear that bell rung. If Jack Charlton enjoyed his solitude he was to have hours, days and weeks of it here.

The favourite pastime

"Is that all I'm going to be doing all day?" he asked. "Yes." "On me own?" "Yes." "For the rest of me days?" "Yes." "Nah. I doon't wunt that. Where's the manager's office?"

At fifteen years of age Charlton stalked to the pit manager's office, marched in and thanked the firm for the sixteen weeks' training and announced he was turning his back on the town's industry. It was John Wayne "the hell I will" sort of stuff and must have kept the town gossips busy for weeks. All of Ashington must have waited, half-longing for Jack Charlton to fall flat on his face after that. For the son of a miner living in a mining town it was a momentous decision. He'd wanted to see the inside of a mine and having been there he'd changed his mind. Imagine. At fifteen he was cut off from mining and trapped in the footballing shadow of his younger brother.

The doughtiness of the boy lives on in the man, though. Jack Charlton grasped long ago that life is too short and too valuable to spend doing those things that he doesn't like or staying in those places where he isn't wanted. He has always left without being asked, so free of lingering regret that the

Jack Charlton indoctrinating his children at an early age.

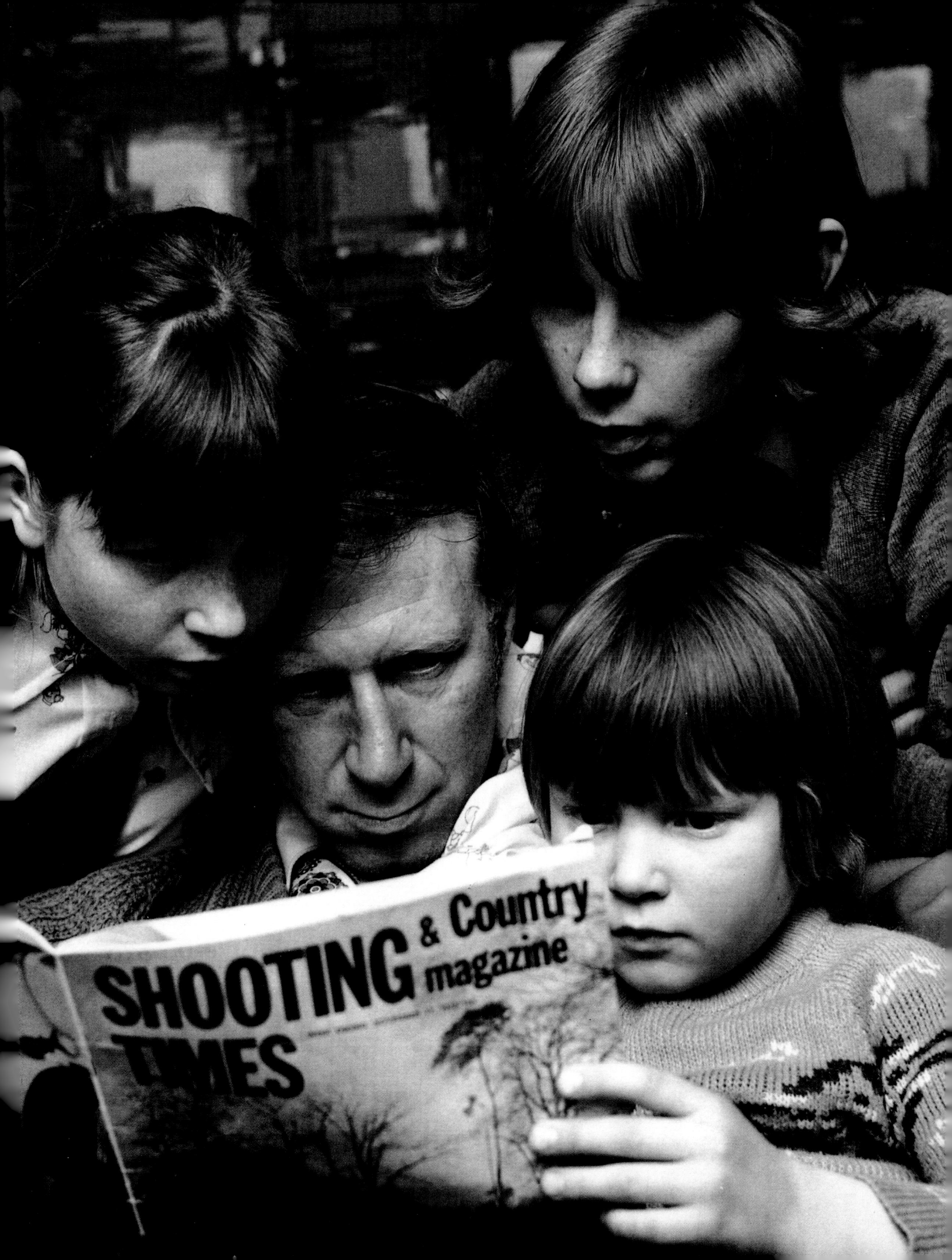
& Country
SHOOTING
magazine
TIMES

A heroes' welcome in Ashington. After the 1966 World Cup victory, Jack and Bobby cruise through their home town in a 1926 Rolls Royce.

door never touches his backside on the way out. Mining, Ashington, Leeds United, Middlesbrough, Sheffield Wednesday, Newcastle – the pattern of departure has always been the same.

When Jack Charlton witnessed his great friend Jock Stein die while watching an international football match some years ago he became fond of telling the world that he wasn't going to die at a football match, that he might die being dragged by a trout down the Tweed but he wouldn't die at a football match. Stein's death had left its mark but the philosophy which Charlton subsequently expounded had its roots in the dust and grime of

Linton. Life was too short and its pleasures too sweet to permit oneself to become prematurely stooped, condemned to ramble the streets as a wheezing bag of bones.

To football then. It was in the very air at the time, a sudden infinity of possibilities. Newcastle were on the crest of their great revival, on the cusp of bringing home some silverware in the early summer of 1951. Jack Charlton, scouting for a start in life, conscious that a miner's son who turns his back on the mines has few chances left, earned an interview for a police cadetship at Morpeth and a trial for Leeds United at Elland

Road on the same day. His head dragged him towards the police interview but his heart, his instincts, which have seldom betrayed him, brought him to Leeds, where he played at full-back for the afternoon and was asked to leave his signature on some apprentice forms before he left. Three days later he left home.

Eighteen clubs were in heat, sniffing around for the signature of his brother Bobby at the same time. One offered to double the best offer Bobby received, regardless of amount. The retinue trailing after Bobby to school games became so overwhelming that the local education authorities were forced to object. The effect on Jack meanwhile of having to bundle himself quietly off to unfashionable, dowdy Leeds to learn the trade is difficult to calculate. Some measure of it is gleaned by the ferocity with which he contests any suggestion of jealousy, by the lengths he will go to deprecate himself.

> "I was a clogger. He was a footballer. I knew that. I had to work."

"I could never be jealous of our kid. Never. He was different to me, another creature. We always knew he would be great. Everyone in Ashington knew it. He could play. I could only stop people playing. I was a clogger. He was a footballer. I knew that. I had to work."

In the end, time and success and personality differences drove Jack and Bobby apart. Back then, though, if there were cracks they were papered over. Jack might have been a clogger and a scyther (the only one in that case to have become Footballer of the Year, an honour he stole in 1967, a year later than Bobby) but the decades have revealed Jack to be the more substantial individual, the more authoritative personality. Jack never had to suffer the risk of being made callow by instant success. He has led two separate lives, each splashed with football glory, and in the long autumn of his football days seems closer to true self-fulfilment than most men whose working time is drawing to a close.

Ashington, and the brief sojourn down the mines and the subsequent death of that industry left Jack Charlton with a deep appreciation of the value of fellowship and community. The Irish team he has managed since 1986 has had its dissi-

dents and its noteworthy rows, but that sense of solidarity has been stitched in. The team are tight. Back in the early fifties, signing on as an apprentice Charlton wasn't even only vaguely aware of the distance he would travel in the beautiful game. He was content to be a relatively anonymous link in the family football chain. His Uncle Jimmy was still a journeyman pro at Leeds when Jack arrived as a groundsboy. Young Bobby was on the threshold of stardom. Two years later Jack would sign on as professional for the same standard £10 fee that Wor Jackie had received when signing on for Newcastle. If the family torch was being passed on to another generation nobody cared much about Jack Charlton's part in grasping it.

Only Cissie had called it correctly. Bringing her eldest, the newborn Jack Charlton back to Beatrice Street in May 1935 she had been stopped by a neighbour enquiring after the little bruiser's health. "Eee," said Cissie, "the bairn's lovely and his feet are fine, too."

Charlton takes aim. Memories of an earlier life, on a rifle range with the Middlesboro FC in 1974.

CHAPTER TWO

YEARS OF GROWTH

At Leeds United, Charlton's growth mirrored that of the club. The tall centre-half was a plodding labourer through his second-division days, but the revitalizing influence of Don Revie transformed Charlton into a polished artisan ready to make the breakthrough with England as he approached thirty.

(Previous pages) 'Me, I was a clogger, I stopped them playing...' Charlton marks Liverpool's Hateley, August 1968.

He's a north of England football man then, the whole rough wrapped package. Some part of him is rooted permanently in that era of brilliantined outside rights and flat-capped Saturday crowds and Movietone World Cups and Walnut plugs and Capstans. Charlton has his critics who would say that everything he knows about football he learned back then, that not a new idea has trespassed in his brain since he passed his mid twenties. He has his advocates, too, who claim that he enjoys putting out that image, that this football brain never sleeps. "When Jack Charlton fishes," says Johann Cruyff, "he thinks about football."

Whatever the ongoing state of the learning process the most intensive tutorials took place at Elland Road through the fifties. At that time Leeds was a Rugby League town. Soccer struggled to stay alive. The Leeds United which Charlton arrived at was a dowdy second-division outfit which in a given season had as much chance of going down a division as they had of going up a grade.

Money came his way. The first wage he had ever earned looked after itself in accounting terms. Four pounds a week came his way, he sent a pound home. He spent £2.50 on digs and the remainder he took due care with. In his first two years at Leeds he remembers visiting the city centre just once.

Because he is gruff and flat-capped and hails from the north of England people like to join the dots and find in Charlton evidence of meanness and parsimony, a man who hoards his brass obsessively. Customarily in Ireland stinginess has been a capital offence, entire clans have been forced to emigrate rather than face the shame of being related to someone who fails to buy their round of drinks in a saloon bar. With Jack Charlton, though, this perceived tightness is considered a

Brothers. Jack and Bobby leave PFA meeting, November 1960.

Handsome is as handsome does. Jack with the England squad, May 1965.

mark of his intelligence and fine breeding, a forgivably English trait. If you sent Jack out on the town with a tenner in his pocket he'd arrive home drunk in a taxi with £20 in his wallet they say admiringly.

Charlton works hard certainly and drives a bargain with relish but one detects that it is the sheer process of earning money which he enjoys rather than the lonely thrill of hoarding it. There are no symptoms to suggest miserliness. No reason to suppose that the big mouth curls up with pleasure as he opens his biscuit tins full of cash every evening and commences counting. The evidence, objectively examined, suggests not meanness but a characteristic Geordie mistrust of anything or anyone too flash. Charlton retains four houses, one in Ireland, one in Spain and one at home in Northumberland, another in Yorkshire plus another he provided for his mother Cissie before she took to the nursing home in her eighties. His quiet moments of generosity are largely undocumented. The disabled anglers trust and the striking miners in the eighties have been notable beneficiaries.

His generosity operates on a more personal level, too. After the European championships in 1988 when the Irish had made their exit and the adrenalin had stopped pumping Charlton encountered a senior Irish soccer journalist in the lobby of the hotel. Pleasantries were exchanged and the journalist professed himself to be shattered with tiredness, knackered. Charlton dipped into his pocket and produced a set of keys. "The house in Spain. Take as long as you want there." He may not be Albert Schweitzer but Charlton has his moments.

In the fifties the need to earn money, the habit and ethic of honest earning was just manifesting itself. Charlton by his own account "would do anything to earn money". Nothing sleazy, mind. "Back then I used to go with the third team to their Yorkshire league matches, because more often than not one of the linesmen wouldn't turn up and if that happened you got ten bob for running the line. It was a regular event that all three officials wouldn't turn up. I always went along. Anything to earn a few quid. I stuck at it a few years, worked very hard really."

Life at a struggling Yorkshire football club in the fifties had the virtue of keeping a lad ego free. Charlton earned his £4 a week as ground-staff boy back in the days when the ground staff consisted almost exclusively of boys. They were the cheap labour upon which football clubs propelled themselves onwards. Ground-staff boys were the lowest level on the scale of professional footballing evolution. Jack Charlton swept the terraces after Saturday games and cleaned the boots of senior players in the mornings. He cleaned the toilets and mopped the dressing-room floors and tended to all the jobs necessary to the existence of a small dowdy second-division Yorkshire football club.

Leeds was a no-frills club in a no-frills division. The two-year term Jack embarked upon was deemed to be an apprenticeship but was in fact a footballing self-help course. Coaching was considered effete. A boy just picked up whatever he could by watching and imitating the seniors. During the summers, the apprentice players had their time. Free from the cleaning and scraping duties that regular attendances would bequeath them the apprentices would play football all day long in the lee of the main stand.

The schedule in season was unvarying. Training consisted of a magical and time-honoured formula: run the long side of the pitch, jog the short side, run the long side, jog the short side. Some padding would have been needed if Leeds were ever to have entertained serious thoughts about producing a work-out video. The entire playing staff ran the long side and jogged the short side endlessly until they were deemed fit and ready. Then the seniors would wander out through the Elland Road stand and play a full game on the cinder car park outside. A corner of the car park was reserved for the apprentices, who would be tossed a ball and left to their own devices. Charlton plugged away uncomplainingly with the herd, distinguishing himself by virtue of being the only giraffe in the company and by wearing a major hairdo the like of which would not be seen again until Rick Astley made his breakthrough. Jack was an emperor of the air.

Back then you learned the truth at seventeen.

First cap. New-boy Jack with Bobby before England début v Scotland, April 1965.

Charlton had only twenty years and another 628 league games to go before retirement beckoned.

35

FA Cup Final, v Liverpool, 1 May 1965. Jackie Charlton concedes a corner as Gary Sprake sells an elaborate dummy.

On 8 May 1952, his seventeenth birthday, Jack Charlton duly got the news. "I've been told," said Arthur Crowther, "to sign you as a professional." The club's manager Major Frank Buckley and the entire senior squad were away on a post-season tour at the time. Charlton at a loose end and with nobody to tell the good news to wandered into the confectioner's across the road and announced that he was now a pro. Over the counter came the news that such a turn of events was little surprise, half a dozen clubs had been keeping an eye on Charlton anyway, popping into the sweetshop occasionally for reports on his progress from behind the counter. Jack wandered out into the Leeds morning, the great loping strides carrying just the hint of a swagger.

He had his £10 signing-on fee fresh in his pocket and had been signed in a gesture of unprecedented Yorkshire generosity by Leeds on the maximum wage of £18 15s. They could have got Charlton for over £6 a week less but what they bought with the extra few pounds was not just the player but his great well of loyalty.

> **Revie was an astute football man who made the most out of limited means, an example Charlton never forgot.**

He made his senior début the following April in a glamour-spangled end-of-season second-division game of absolutely no importance to anybody but the gangly Leeds centre-half who managed to get his head or toe to most things through the ninety minutes. When the long whistle blew the Uniteds of Leeds and Doncaster had a goal apiece and Jack Charlton had only twenty years and another 628 league games to go before retirement beckoned.

He might even have played more games than that but for the interruption which military service brought the following season. A spell in the Royal Horse Guards deprived him of an entire season at Leeds and the opportunity to work during his first season with a newly installed manager, Raich Carter, a legend of north-eastern football. Army life was good and pleasant, though. The hairstyle was downloaded but Jack transpired still to be over six foot tall and was sent to the Guards at Windsor where he became the first player from outside the officers' mess to captain

the Horse Guards soccer team. He organised training and made sure his players were looked after well. "Late breakfasts and lots of cushy jobs." His side won the Cavalry Cup in Germany and when in September 1954 Charlton was demobbed that remained the sole honour he had gleaned in action. "If I'm not in the first team by the end of the season, I'll pack in it in," Jack told himself, heading back for Leeds.

Of all people it was John Charles who made the room for Charlton to become a fixture in the first squad, the bulky Welshman moving from centre-half to centre-forward in one of those desperate football gambles which occasionally throw out a jackpot. John Charles scored forty-two league goals that season. He was generous with his time, too, John Charles. He'd show Jack things, revelations. Literally he opened young Charlton's eyes. "He taught me how to head a ball with me eyes open. He was a wonderful header of the ball. We all closed our eyes out of reflex. He showed me how to head the ball where I wanted to head it. He was as strong as an ox you know John Charles. As strong as an ox."

He taught other things too, tricks of the trade, the secrets of the footballing freemasonry. How to

kill the ball on the chest. How to take it down on the thigh and turn it in the direction you were headed. How to sell the centre-forward a dummy before he sells one to you.

"When he's running at you, you go forward as if you are coming to tackle him, then check back and go the way he's running so you match his run. He's pushed it the way you want him to push it when he's seen you come and you've got a yard or two start on him anyway. You'll get him."

Leeds gained promotion from Division Two as runners up in the 1955–56 season and Charlton had little difficulty adjusting to the higher grade of football. The team plodded through the late fifties, fatally content with its lot. The players were still running the long side and jogging the short side of the Elland Road pitch. In the 1959–60 season, with a forlorn inevitability they were relegated once again. John Charles had departed to Juventus and the side were effectively leaderless. In the bad times, as the drop became unavoidable, Bill Lambton, who had succeeded Raich Carter as manager, was in turn succeeded by Jack Taylor, a Yorkshireman who had played successfully with Sunderland and was gaining a somewhat dangerous reputation about the leagues as somebody who liked to think about the game. Leeds with plenty to think about themselves decided Taylor was worth the risk. Jack Charlton, who was growing stale and bored with football, appreciated the new celebration which swept Elland Road.

Taylor may have been a thinker, but he was dangerous too. Here's how Jack in his mid twenties learned the art of kicking a ball properly: "He would lay down two bricks and put the ball between them and ask you to run up and hit it full on. Aye, you'd be a bit tentative at first but you soon learned to keep your eye on the ball."

During Taylor's two years in charge Don Revie arrived as a player from Manchester City and when Taylor shuffled off with his hod and ball Revie succeeded him at the helm. During his time as a coach he had told Charlton that his performances were so listless that were he in charge he would drop him. Revie brought two first-class coaches with him, Syd Owen and Les Cocker, both graduates and evangelists of the burgeoning Lilleshall school of soccer thought. Jack Charlton decided that the time had come to banish his listlessness and begin learning again.

When nearly three decades later Leeds manager

Another league title race with Leeds, May 1966.

Howard Wilkinson purchased the elderly and decrepit Gordon Strachan from Manchester United and re-energised him to bring Leeds out of the second division Wilkinson was hailed as a visionary. In fact he is just a man who understands history. Revie purchased an even more elderly and diminutive Scottish midfield player from Everton and gave him the kiss of life. Bobby Collins was thirty-one when Revie bought him in March 1962 and unable to gain a first-team place at Goodison Park. Over the following three or four years he became one of the greatest midfielders in Britain, was recalled to the Scottish national side after an absence of six years and was chosen as Footballer of the Year in the 1964–65 season.

Collins possessed a demonic will to win which infected Charlton and the remainder of Revie's side for the duration of their time as one of England's great club sides. Even after Collins had moved on to another phase of the long twilight of his career across the border with Morton his guts and determination were spoken about as being the genus of the Leeds attitude. That attitude led certain younger members of the squad to cross certain boundaries of fair play and decency in their pursuit of success, but Charlton always remained a tough and scrupulously fair professional.

Revie was an astute football man who made the most out of limited means, an example Charlton never forgot. He purchased a disenchanted Johnny Giles from Manchester United on 30 August 1963 and the historic revival had its final component in place. Leeds finished the 1963–64 season as comfortable second-division

Dig this: Jack opens his men's-wear shop in Garforth Leeds, 1966.

champions, going on to make an immediate impression on the first division by finishing second in the following two seasons.

The only fly in the ointment in those early Revie days had been Charlton. Before his accession to the manager's chair, Revie had been critical of the big Geordie and now as one of the senior players Jack couldn't resist the constant urge to speak out against every perceived injustice inflicted on the group by Revie. Finally under threat of being transferred Charlton settled down to the business of learning his trade from scratch.

Jack Charlton was by now a professional of some ten years standing and with the departure of Bobby Collins at that time he became the senior player at the club. Still he dogged the shadow of his brother Bobby, who had been capped for England before the age of twenty-one. The brothers were close then. Jack has often recalled the pattern of weekends off when Bobby would call Jackie on his way home to Ashington from Manchester via Leeds and the older brother would join the train and together they would travel back to their home. When Bobby prospered and purchased a car he would stop off at Leeds and drive Jack and his new wife

Pat home, all three together and contented. Jack was with Bobby on the afternoon when the younger brother learned that at twenty he was about to win the first of his 106 caps for England. "We came out of a cinema and bought a newspaper and there it was in the stop press. We let out a whoop. We stood there in the street celebrating. I was delighted for him. Delighted."

It has been said that the Munich air crash in February 1958 changed Bobby. It would be surprising if such a traumatic experience didn't leave some scarring. Jack remembers being in a dressing room when the news came through, some clown running in and breathlessly announcing the news to the whole Leeds contingent, bawling that there were no survivors. None. And then as if in slow motion the realisation dawned on the roomful of players that Big Jack's brother was on the plane and the place fell silent.

Jack's instinct told him to go home. He collected his wife Pat and together they journeyed to Newcastle on the train. All the long way back the carriages murmured with talk of Munich and the bodies lying there on the iced runway. In the Haymarket in Newcastle the news of Bobby was good. Jack swears to this day that he read the eight-point type in the stop-press column from yards away. "Bobby Charlton among the survivors." That sentence screamed at him as if it were a headline. He continued to Ashington anyway, home to Beatrice Street, there to absorb the loss of fellow professionals, friends and colleagues who had attended Jack and Pat's wedding not long before.

After Munich Bobby may indeed have changed, travelling home less often than before and becoming more obsessive about Manchester United and the game of soccer. The rift between the brothers appears to have come later in life, when past their playing days the brothers needed different things from football and the common ground between them evaporated. Jack Charlton has been criticised more than once for insensitivity in various football-related matters. In the business of family and loyalty and getting through hard times, however, he is a different man, someone who makes allowances. He has defined that border himself. "You can fart about with me all you bloody like, but don't fart about with me if you've got a football at your feet."

Until their mid-thirties the Charlton brothers had always been tied and moulded by common

*Away with
Leeds*

experience: Ashington, family, school, football, early hair loss. The cloistered life of football suspends a person's development in many ways. As they grew and developed in their lives after football Jack and Bobby became different people. There is no row, no bone of contention to pick over and analyse in the search for a brother to blame. Just a separateness.

In 1965, at any rate, things were still tight between the brothers. Leeds's insanely competitive young side were hacking it up in the first division, chasing Manchester United all the way for the championship and Cup double. Leeds's hard-tackling and methodical style was drawing criticism from many quarters. Leeds and Everton, for instance, always had their problems. Once with Charlton stationed like a turret on his goal-line the Everton goalkeeper Gordon West put his hands over Jack's face. If West couldn't see the ball, Jack wasn't going to see it either. Jack responded by attempting to take a bite out of West's hand.

> **Jack scored seventy league goals in his time with Leeds, most of them headers at the near post.**

In November 1964 the problems were more conventional than that of players eating each other. A league game against Everton had to be abandoned for ten minutes to allow the players and fans to calm down following a series of incidents and brawls. The following month's league game at Old Trafford, however, established Leeds as a footballing as well as a bodily threat, Bobby Collins scoring the winning goal in a game that served as the starting pistol for an enthralling league race, between Leeds, Manchester United and Chelsea.

While Chelsea's campaign went adrift on a tide of indiscipline the two northern clubs coveted the league and Cup double. With the league still hanging in the balance Leeds and Manchester United clashed in the FA Cup semi-final at Hillsborough early in April 1965. The game was a scoreless draw, but the excitement came in the form of the brawls and bouts of ill-temper which punctuated the action. The referee Dick Windle surrendered control early on and players created and enforced their own rules. Denis Law and Jack Charlton scuffled on the edge of the Leeds penalty

**1967
Footballer of
the Year**

The magnitude of his trespass was just beginning to dawn on Jack. "Ah, great," replied Bobby at length. "Now, fuck off out of here," came another voice. "That," says Jack years later, "is the sort of tact I am famous for."

Looking back now, that season for Leeds was nothing but more of the same old story. They went on to lose a key league match to Manchester United at Elland Road on 17 April and then lost again to Sheffield Wednesday two days later, that end-of-season brittleness that would always haunt them making its first appearance. The pendulum swung Old Trafford's way again and the league title was won by Manchester United on goal aggregate on the final day of the season despite their surprise loss to Aston Villa. In May, Leeds lost the FA Cup final to Liverpool in extra time and Jack Charlton's bottom drawer began to fill up with loser's medals.

He might have become a fixture on the runners-up podium but Charlton was reborn as a footballer in the early to mid sixties. Most afternoons were taken up with skills practice at Elland Road. Charlton remembers hours on end heading away balls tossed in the air by Les Cocker or Syd Owen. His own interest in coaching began to develop. He went to Lilleshall and took his coaching badges. In the mornings before arriving at training for Leeds he would coach school teams in the Leeds area, working with the region's coach Jimmy Frew, and a slew of early successes fired his enthusiasm and increased the demand for his services.

The Revie era at Leeds saw a transformation which was reflected at several other top clubs. Players and management would discuss games and tactics endlessly. Set pieces would be practised and worked upon. The sloppy but manful football of the forties and fifties was scorned. Charlton under the guidance of concerned coaches and an enlightened manager revealed himself to be an adept natural reader of the game and an intelligent and agile centre-half. His Irish teams have always played the game with a simple directness and an adherence to rudimentary precepts of the game that has baffled and irked footballing nations with more aching pretensions to greatness. If the Irish appliance of footballing science is a little dated it is because the chief chemist graduated when the theories were still being empirically tested. While testing continued Jack Charlton liked what he saw and went with his hunch that it would work. He has been unshakeable ever since.

area, the shirt almost being torn off Law's back. When years later Jack Charlton, in all likelihood exaggerating, stated that he retained a little black book containing the names of the players he intended to "do" Law asserted confidently that his was the only name in the book.

The replay at the City Ground Nottingham four days later was marginally more temperate and Leeds carved out a 1-0 win with a goal wholly against the run of play three minutes from the end. Billy Bremner headed home a John Giles free kick and for the remainder of the game the Manchester defence bitterly protested the award of that free kick.

In the Leeds dressing room afterwards with pulses still racing and adrenalin still pumping Don Revie took Jack Charlton aside. Good news. Big Jack, almost twenty-nine years old by then, had been selected at last to play for England. His début was to come in the home championships against Scotland in May. Beaming from ear to ear Charlton jogged straight out of the Leeds dressing room and into the stunned seething silence of the Manchester United dressing room. Brother Bobby was slumped in a corner examining his bootlaces. Manchester United's entire season seemed to have turned that afternoon. Leeds had gained a Cup Final place and a psychological edge in the battle for the league title. "Hey, our kid," boomed Big Jack merrily, "I'm in the England team." Silence.

*Jack explains
away a hefty
tackle, England
v Wales, 1969.*

Charlton, Bremner and Giles. Leeds United, 1968.

to Jack, who greatly enjoyed the little piece of grandstanding and notoriety which the corner-kick tactic involved. Jack duly took umbrage and refused to go upfield for corners for six or seven months. Defences all over Britain celebrated the resumption of business as usual. Finally in the battle of wills Don Revie lost and decreed that another Leeds player should move into the centre-half position while Jack performed his party piece at the opposite end of the field. The Lowryesque splinter that was Big Jack began appearing on opposition goal-lines again. Willingly though in the battle with Revie the big man would have sacrificed his nose to spite his face.

In February 1966, not long before the World Cup was to make him an English folk hero, Big Jack's corner-kick antics led him into another fine mess. A Fairs Cup game with Valencia was abandoned for several minutes as a result of a fist fight.

He was central to the tactical innovation for which Leeds became most notorious. When his side won a corner kick Charlton would amble up to the opposition goal-line and station himself at the near post facing the kicker. The big centre-half would then be positioned right in the line of vision of the opposing goalie. With the keeper now unsighted Billy Bremner would stand off the action, behind Charlton, ready to snap at whatever crumbs fell his way by way of breaking balls. For free kicks Charlton would join the opposition defenders on their own goal-line, spreading panic like a fox in a coop. Jack scored seventy league goals in his time with Leeds, most of them headers at the near post. The number of goals he created merely by sowing havoc in the opposition defence is unknown.

Charlton enjoyed the role, with the streak of Geordie bloody-mindedness he always retained, he relished the abuse and the controversy heaped upon him for his part in the use of a perfectly legal tactic. He has always been instinctively anti-authoritarian. Standing on the opposition goal-line was a footballing expression of that stance. Two incidents from that era reveal a lot about the singular truculent man Jack was to become.

The corner-kick tactic was deployed by Leeds with considerable success but Revie tersely noted on more than one occasion that Jack's slow progress in getting back down the field was leaving Leeds exposed at the other end in the event of a quick opposition breakaway. This was pointed out

Charlton's forays on to the opposing goal-line were responsible. Spanish goalkeepers were regarded as a protected species at the time and the sight of Charlton lumbering up and standing directly in front of the keeper was deemed an offence to all the Valencians held sacred. For his profanity Charlton was spat at, elbowed, kicked and scratched. Seventeen minutes from full time, however, and the chemical balance in Jack's brain went awry. Sinned against one time too many by the Valencia defender Vidagany, Charlton turned to issue his own retribution. Vidagany, who in all likelihood had a wife and children whom he hoped one day to see again, turned heel and ran. Big Jack came loping after Vidagany, chasing him slapstick fashion across the Elland Road turf bellowing insults and threats like a giraffe coursing a hare. Finally the giraffe caught the Spaniard with a right hook. Blows were traded freely. The craze

caught on. Both teams had to be dragged from the field. When they re-emerged ten minutes later from their dressing rooms Charlton and Vidagany were left behind.

Such strokes of odd drama were expected of Jack Charlton. Apart from being the senior player in the Leeds squad he enjoyed a reputation for being a little apart from the rest of the group, a separation which was accentuated by his mild eccentricities of dress and manner and by the age difference between him and the rest of the group. He recognises it himself looking back through the years. As with money and earning he enjoyed the process of playing more than the rewards of playing.

"I never needed it, the celebration, the people everywhere. I can enjoy it, but I don't need it. Not the way some players need it. You know in here," and he will tap his temple, "you know in here what you have done and how you have done it."

Terrorising Wolves. Charlton in league action, September 1968.

CHAPTER THREE

BEYOND THE SIDELINES

Charlton's long period as a player led, almost inevitably, to a career in club management. His first job took him home to the north-east, to the floundering empire that was Middlesboro FC. His straightforward football philosophy met with instant success on the field, and his convictions grew unshakeable.

*(Previous
pages) Boss of
Middlesboro,
man of the
times.*

The notion of Jack Charlton being set apart from his fellow players falls easily into the pattern of his playing days. When he was in his mid-twenties in the Leeds side he was already the senior player at the club, developing relationships with manager and coaches rather than with the great group of players behind him snapping at his heels. By the time he came to play for England he was twenty-nine and already notorious for his corner-kick routine and for being the less talented, less bald older brother of Bobby. He came into an England establishment where the younger Charlton was already the star and where most of the group was again younger than him. He never quite experienced the giddiness of being young and successful with the football world at his feet. Jack Charlton indeed isn't a man whom one would lightly accuse of ever having experienced giddiness.

It was interesting to watch Charlton at press conferences during the US World Cup standing aside or at the back of the room as three of his

prodigies Jason McAteer, Phil Babb and Gary Kelly performed for the media. Jack would watch them intently, all the while his eyes flicking from his players to the media, wondering at the sheer lightness of it all. He would encourage the three in their enjoyment of the tournament, prompting them to buy masks and wigs for press conferences and permitting them to enjoy a remarkable amount of media exposure. That lightness of being had eluded Charlton as a young footballer. The three amigos became a strange media phenomenon during the US World Cup, indulged in their enjoyment by Charlton. "Oooh, look, it's Bobbee Charlton," roared Phil Babb excitedly one morning as Charlton strode beetle-browed across the press interview room. The media erupted. Charlton permitted himself a broad almost paternal smile. So that's what it would have been like. That's how it was for Bobby.

The general Charlton antipathy towards the media grew out of the Leeds era. For all their hard football and determination Leeds were constantly pilloried for their lack of style and surfeit of grit

Another triumph: Don Revie and Jack Charlton at Elland Road.

and ugliness. The team and players took a perverse pleasure in their unpopularity. When finally in 1967 they won a trophy, the League Cup (by a single goal when Charlton ran interference on Arsenal keeper Jim Furnell following an Eddie Gray corner; Furnell fumbled and Terry Cooper turned the resultant bobble to the net), the media backlash was immense. Leeds were condemned for their dull "method play". Charlton, who for fifteen years with Leeds as a professional had toiled without winning a major trophy, now found himself the whipping boy for the media in his moment of victory. He was castigated severely for his positioning on the Arsenal goal-line and for some weeks the controversy burned on with rent-an-opinion mangers and columnists calling for the rule regarding players positioning for corner kicks to be changed. The label "soccer cheat" was bandied about hurtfully in some quarters.

From 1964 onwards when the media championed Manchester United for the title over the newly promoted underdogs from Leeds, the

Revie management group and players exhibited an extraordinary collective paranoia regarding the media. The harsher the criticism of their style became the greater Leeds's devotion to their brand of football became. That quality has remained with Charlton ever since. When delicate, quivering aesthetes have written about the perceived sterility of Ireland's long-ball game Charlton has derived a perverse pleasure from the criticism. When at last in 1994 Niall Quinn's likely absence from the World Cup through injury allied to the surfeit of quality midfielders at his disposal forced Charlton to switch to a more measured passing game in the guise of a 4-5-1 formation he couldn't stand to concede the victory to his erstwhile critics. That's the way we have always played, he insisted.

It wasn't but that's just the way Jack has always been. The story is related of Jack having a quiet read of his paper in a toilet stall at Elland Road one morning after training. A bucket of ice-cold water is tossed prankishly over the door. Charlton emerges freezing cold but fuming, dripping from head to foot and holding between each thumb

In front of the camera, September 1971.

and forefinger a little soggy remnant of his newspaper. Red-faced and quivering, he excoriates his team-mates for their immaturity, pointing the finger at various suspects he takes a Sicilian-style oath of revenge. "Anyway," he bellows as he stalks out leaving puddles behind him, "you missed." Same old stubborn Jack. Not given to idle frivolity. He deeply distrusts ostentation; he prefers burlap to silk.

In the days when Mick McCarthy patrolled the Irish defence with the touch and pace of an enthused rhino, the press corps would pass long nights debating the topic of when Jack Charlton would see through McCarthy. Not until some forward skins him and Ireland lose an important game by a hatful was the consensus opinion. And when that happened Jack would be to blame. Nobody in the company would have the slightest

Warm-up v Sheffield United, 1972.

George Cohen defends while Jack offers assistance, World Cup Final, 1966.

hesitation in telling Jack that either. It never happened. Mick McCarthy, the immensely likeable Barnsley man, played them all – Hagi, Lineker, Gullit, Schillachi, Van Basten and more. He never got skinned. "My record for juggling," McCarthy used to say, "is sixty kicks without it tipping the ground. But that was with a centre-forward."

Charlton persevered with McCarthy and will in the future persevere with Alan Kernaghan because Charlton doesn't rate centre-half play as being one of the higher sciences and because he likes the virtues McCarthy and Kernaghan bring to the pack: honesty, intelligence, courage, those qualities he perceives himself as possessing. About centre-

half play Charlton was always straightforward. He told Bobby Moore when he arrived in the England team that he, Jack, would play everything, attack everything. When he won the ball he'd give it to a white shirt. Anything more fancy or ambitious Mr Moore could look after for himself.

"You don't stress yourself too much at centre-half," Charlton is on the record as saying, "the ball comes to you when you are facing it and you get rid of it to one of your own men. Keep it simple, that's all."

Under the simple dogmas expounded by Alf Ramsey, Charlton found international football easier to play than club football. Ramsey wanted

assumed by caption writers the world over to be offering up a prayer of thanks. That journalistic brush stroke was too flashy and melodramatic for his Geordie sensibilities, though, and he professed afterwards to kneeling because he was "bloody knackered". He has the photograph of the moment at home but is quick to stress that "It's not hanging up, like, it's somewhere about the house. I don't know where." At the end of the game Jack was dry-eyed while his brother Bobby wept and their parents in the stands hollered and cheered. The differing reactions appeared to define the brothers in the public eye. Jack Charlton might have been up there where the air is rare that day but he seems curiously unaffected by the experience. He takes the view that it was all part of the process of being a professional. Something other than football defines Jack Charlton.

Many of that England team have been notable ever since for their inability to cope with life's sheer dullness, for their inability to grow into the men that their legend demanded they should be. Their stories are suffused with drink and bitterness and bankruptcy. One pictures them watching the

Beaten brothers. Jack and Bobby return from the 1970 Mexico World Cup.

his players to learn and perform simple functions which would become second nature to them. Years later as an international manager on his first away trip with the team, to a triangular tournament in Iceland, Charlton would sit his players down and enunciate a list of functions he wanted them to learn and perform. Simple, one function per man. With the best midfielders in the league protecting him and waiting to relieve him of possession the game of the centre-half was reduced to its purest form for Jack. Watch and swoop, watch and swoop, right to the top.

At the end of his greatest playing day Jack Charlton knelt on the Wembley turf and was video of their greatest moments over and over again, the glow of the Technicolored sixties footage freakishly illuminating their faces as they watch in the suburban darkness, mouthing every word of Wolstenholmes's commentary. "They think it's over...it is now." Rewind.

Of that team only Jack Charlton's personality has grown and developed sufficiently for the World Cup not to have become a burden. For Jack the experience of rewatching those 120 minutes of English glory on video for the first time last year appears to have left him strangely unmoved. "The ninety minutes was very little really," he says of the game's opening acts. He has a defender's vivid flashes of memory about the goals and about rearguard mix-ups throughout the game. Memories,

By the 1973 FA Cup Final Charlton was already establishing a career as a TV pundit.

too, of his friend Bobby Moore waltzing his way out of danger late in extra time and sweeping the ball majestically forward.

At the end Charlton ran the length of the ground to embrace Geoff Hurst, who sold him a quick dummy and forced Charlton to chase after him again. By the time Hurst was in receipt of a big Geordie hug Charlton was dead on his feet. The world would be keen to know the precise nature of the gruff endearments Big Jack whispered into Hurst's ear at that moment, but both parties claim to have forgotten. If Charlton made extravagantly romantic promises to the starry-eyed Hurst he can be forgiven. Jack had other things on his mind that afternoon besides football. The next day as England fumbled for a hangover cure Charlton was on the road back to home and Pat, who was expecting their youngest son.

Strangely for a man of such dramatically dogmatic views on life Jack retains a charming belief in the power of superstition. He liked to be last out of the Leeds dressing room during the great days and wouldn't leave those confines without first heading a football ten times to Norman

'Don't recognise me with me clothes on, do ye?' Jack after Leeds FA Cup semi-final win over Wolves, April 1973.

Hunter. Talk of the World Cup and his early exit from the celebrations in 1966 sparks another memory in him. He missed the birth of his first son John through football. His daughter Debbie arrived while he was at a course in Lilleshall. When Peter was finally due, the two eldest were sent to Cissie's Northumberland home for a week. Jack took himself off out of town briefly. "I hadn't been there for the first ones, so it was lucky for us. Silly really but...I came back, came back to see the kid an all."

His career on the playing fields petered out slowly in the late sixties. Jack went to the 1970 World Cup finals in Mexico with England and played against Czechoslovakia early on but was

dropped for the remainder of the competition. He still maintains that Ramsey was wrong to leave him on the bench, that he could have done a good job against West Germany, in particular at the semi-final stage.

In truth 1970 had been a long and tiring year for a thirty-five-year-old player. Leeds had endured one of those long vaguely heroic English league seasons where they tilted at every wind-mill, with their by now customary lack of success. By mid-March they had played fifty-two games, losing only three times. By the end of the season they had gone on to surrender the league, the European Cup and the FA Cup and play almost seventy games. The heat of the Mexico World

The long good-bye. Jack's Leeds testimonial, May 1973 – in front of 34,000 fans.

Receiving the OBE with his wife Pat, son John and daughter Debbie, November 1974.

pundit, a creature who would crop up before, during and after football matches and explain what was happening. One of those inventions that nobody thought they needed until it came along. Charlton was the best of them. A frank and fearless critic of players and teams he was the star of the show with Malcolm Allison performing ably in the support role. Compulsive watching.

His profile as a World Cup winner and television personality and genuine son of the northeast attracted the attention of Middlesbrough football club, one of those outfits that perennially populate the second division, a club that thought they deserved better but feared they might end up with worse. Middlesbrough then were much as they are today, stuck in the second division, seeking a ride to the first on the coat-tails of a big name in his first management job, making plans for a new stadium and in the process of becoming one of England's biggest clubs.

Charlton was invited for an interview at Ayresome Park. The first job interview of his life. Thirty-eight years on this earth hadn't equipped him for that sort of ordeal, however. Footballers generally aren't big on the subtleties of personnel recruitment sessions and the nuances of job interview politics. Charlton approached Don Revie about his future and about his interview. Revie sought to persuade Charlton to stay at Elland Road for another two years, but sensing the big man's boredom with playing, he fitted Jack out with a list of requirements which he should ensure were in place before he took the job. The sort of things that football managers learn as they go along: rights, privileges, chain of command, budgets, etc.

One can picture the scene at Middlesbrough as they waited for their star interviewee to arrive. A little knot of suited men drawn from club and community waiting for their afternoon with Jack Charlton. Plans being made as to how the interview shall unfold. What the chairman will say as he opens the discussions, when the local alderman should intervene, how the treasurer should approach the thorny question of money. They file

Cup was probably no place for Charlton to attempt to discover the precise toll those exertions had taken on him.

Later that year the little scandal of the "black book" arose. Jack, probably using an apocryphal story to reveal some of the realities of the professional game, stated that he maintained a little black book in which he kept the names of transgressors with whom he intended to get even on the football pitch. Jack's facility for remembering names is such that he might well need a little black book for such purposes. One summer many years later when his Irish players opted by vote to tour the US instead of Brazil in an off-season tour he reminded them that they were passing up the opportunity to play in the world-famous "marijuana stadium". The English FA retails a different more sanitised version of football, however, and didn't view Jack with the same indulgent affection as the Irish do. He never played for England again. Famously when he applied for the English management job later in the seventies Charlton, the hero of 1966, never received a reply.

By the 1973 FA Cup final which Charlton missed due to a hamstring injury he was already establishing a career as a TV pundit, playing for Leeds in only the big games which got him sufficiently motivated. Between those big games Jack kept himself busy grooming Gordon McQueen as his understudy and eventual replacement.

On television he was the first of a new breed. ITV was just developing the cult of the soccer

Management kept Charlton within the only trade he had ever known.

Managing Middlesboro, 1973.

into the boardroom, arrange themselves as they had planned and wait for Charlton.

When he arrived Charlton was all business and bluster, long and besuited and striding across the room to shake every hand, he pre-empted all questions by slapping his list down on the table and announcing that if he got everything on the list he would take the job. "But, Mr Charlton, this is an interview to ascertain whether or not you will be offered the job." Ah. Realisation. No regrets. "Well, I'm just here to see if I like it enough to take it. I'll wait outside for ten minutes and if you agree to everything on the list I'll be your manager. If not I'll be off and there'll be no harm done."

Middlesbrough were promoted as champions that season, sweeping the second division by a fifteen-point margin while playing the direct and

energetic football preached by their tyro manager Mr Jack Charlton. He stuck, naturally, with simple precepts. Bobby Murdoch arrived as a gift from Jock Stein above in Glasgow. Graham Souness, purchased from the reserve side at Spurs, was converted from tigerish left-back to grinding central midfielder. Alan Foggon, another midfielder and the only player, Charlton says, with whom he has ever had serious difficulties, became the runner and chaser, hurrying off into spaces which the two front runners would create. For all its sweet spontaneity football is played to patterns. Foggon's sheer unpredictability unsettled the best of defences until eventually it too became just another pattern to be dealt with.

Management kept Charlton within the only trade he had ever known but given that lease he

New boss with new jumper. Jack takes over at Newcastle, 1984.

Jack and Kevin Keegan mourn the passing of Don Revie, May 1989.

found himself missing things he didn't expect to miss. The business of transfers and contracts and buying or selling players meant keeping a distance from the playing staff. The society of the dressing room was closed to Charlton for the first time. Once he had enthusiastically worked through his theories on how the game was being played and had seen them unfolding successfully on the pitch much of the thrill evaporated.

Charlton stayed at Middlesbrough through four seasons when the team's early promise never fully bloomed. In 1977 after twenty-seven years of nothing but football he announced he was taking a rest. Middlesbrough owed him nothing but gratitude. The sabbatical lasted for about six months, which one presumes was a period of intense and prolonged tragedy for the trout population of north-east England.

Charlton was lured back into club management later that year by Sheffield Wednesday, a giant not so much sleeping as comatose in the third division. Success didn't come as easily this time, the helter-skelter football of Division Three is a little more difficult to spring suprises on. By 1980 the club were hauled into Division Two, however, and making reasonable if unpretty stabs at reaching the top flight. In 1983, increasingly fed up with the quotidian duties of club management, Charlton called it a day.

At that period only two clubs in Britain could have lured him back into management. Sentimental favourites Leeds or Newcastle United. Leeds were just embarking on their unsuccessful experiment of giving the manager's job to each of the seventies team in turn and Charlton was well down the queue. Newly promoted Newcastle and the stage upon which Wor Jackie had strutted his stuff was an inviting challenge. Jack accepted the job but quickly found himself tied down once more by the lilliputian tasks of club management. The first pre-season cries of "Charlton out" were sufficient for him to clear his desk and leave St James Park behind.

The parting left a bad taste. Newcastle were at that time assembling a group of players to rival anything the club had produced in its long history of underachievement. Beardsley, Waddle and young Paul Gascoigne still in his swaddling clothes were the putative stars. Charlton irked several of the players by dismantling the sweeping style via which they had escaped the badlands of Division Two. Years later when Ireland qualified

for their first World Cup in 1990 Beardsley cropped up in one Sunday newspaper, still evidently peeved at the sort of football he had been asked to play. One aspect of Jack's brief sojourn at Newcastle which bears mention was his tolerant indulgence of young Paul Gascoigne whom at that time was fully submerged in his addiction to Mars bars and the friendship of one Five Bellies Gardner. As with Paul McGrath in later years Charlton found it easy to forgive great talent. Repeatedly Charlton would summon Gascoigne to his office for what was to be the final bust-up over the weight problem and each time Gascoigne left with a grin as broad as a goalmouth and Charlton behind shaking his head indulgently.

In the last few years of his club management career players had noticed Charlton becoming increasingly distracted. Chris Waddle tells a famous story of a car pulling up at the Newcastle training ground one morning and the driver emerging shouting, "Jackie Jackie, there's trout in the Tweed." Charlton swears that the car had come to pick him up to take him to the airport on a scouting trip. "Nobody would tell stories like that if golf was my hobby" he states. The tale, though, is evidence of a growing problem of application and concentration. Not many players can tolerate the blow to the ego that being supplanted in their manager's thoughts by a trout involves.

For the next few years Jack retired to become a part of the celebrity circuit, making long amusing speeches after long rubbery dinners. He kept up a column in the *Daily Express*. Nobody needed to tell him when there was trout in the Tweed.

CHAPTER FOUR

DOGFIGHTS AND DOGMAS

Charlton's appointment as Irish manager was freighted with conspiracy theories and bitter words. It took a string of solid performances and qualification for the 1988 European Championship to transform him from a figure of cult devotion into an object of mass worship.

★★★★★★★★★★★★★★★★★★

(Previous pages) 'Yung people of Ireland, I luff you.' Charlton returns from Italia '90.

He can tell a story. He knows the rituals and the timing. How to draw his audience in. How to paint a character up just right. Where to lay the stress and how to lay the ground for the punch line. He isn't a man for jokes, he likes to mine the comic side of real life. Best of all about his stories is the fact that he savours the telling so much.

He is talking about his mother, Cissie Charlton, mother of all the Charltons, the matriarch. Eighty-two years old and still kicking. He laughs to himself in a way which makes the listener lean forward in anticipation.

"She's a one is Cissie. She's had open-heart surgery, worrying, like, but she's over it now and she's up in a residential home in Newbiggin-by-the-Sea. Nice place. Great sweep of sea outside to look at. There's beaches and the smell of the sea air and walks to be taken and companionship. She likes it there. That's the main thing."

He pushes the pace a little, keen to get to the body of the tale. The speech is littered with Geordie abuse of vowels. "She's an independent buggah, too, yeh neh. Aye, Cissie Charlton. If she can do something on her own she'll do it, or she'll attempt to do it. She has one of those frames but she won't use it. Only if they're looking at her."

He tosses his head back and laughs some more at the good of it. You would have to know this woman, you really would. Anyway, listen to this. He phoned her not long before the World Cup, but before things got really busy. Cissie was skittish with good humour and innocent mischief and over the phone she inveigled a day out for herself and her friend Nora. He made the short drive from Ponteland to Newbiggin and collected them the next day, bundling the pair of them into the

Studying form. Ireland v Hungary 1989.

back of the car in out of a soft drizzle. He'd had an idea for the outing – fish and chips, along the grey coast as far as Amble, the best in the northeast. Like old times for Cissie and Nora, and Jack. He drives. When they arrive Cissie announces that herself and Nora have enjoyed fish and chips just the previous evening.

"Yeh daft buggah," he tells her, chiding softly, "why didn't ya tell me before now?" So he drives onwards to a pub he knows. He likes these parts and the driving is no great chore. He knows this pub and likes its good lunches, nothing fancy, just homely stuff. Good to eat after a day on the river. Anyway, he's taking Cissie out of the car, an operation involving some care, and he has her by the wrist as he leans to shut the door. Suddenly a jet flies overhead. "Whoooshaw," says Jack, conveying the surprise of the airborne intrusion, his flattened hand describing the arc and pace of the overflight. Cissie looks skywards and still being held by the wrist her body takes off in a dainty balletic circle, swivelling out of her son's grip like a ballerina in coat. "Ooooooooheeeeeeeee," she cries pointing skywards, "ooooooheeeeee."

The moment puts Jack's heart crossways. His mother dangling from his grip perilously. He pulls the giggling Cissie to attention. "Yeh silly old buggah," he roars, linking her towards the pub as the upbraiding continues. "Why can't yeh be bloody sensible instead of being so bloody stupid. Yeh could have broke your bloody neck there, woman. Silly, stupid..."

Through the pub door they go and Jack is grumbling and Cissie is laughing and Nora is laughing. Laughing their game old heads off. Exasperated, Jack gets his charges to a seat and deposits them gruffly. Cissie is flopped there in a big high-backed chair and she's laughing and laughing. And Big Jack is standing there glowering and embarrassed. Every eye is on Cissie and Jack. People hereabouts know the Charltons like they know their own relations. At length Cissie's laughing subsides and she gazes about the pub.

"Oooooh," she says to her baited-breath audience. "Oooh, our Jack's a bad-tempered buggah, yeh neh. Eeee's one bad-tempered buggah." The telling is done and his face subsides into laughter. Bad-tempered buggah...

He arrived in Ireland in 1986 and distinguished himself early as a bad-tempered bugger of high pedigree. He lacked *gravitas* and he lacked a feel for Ireland. Most of all he lacked patience. Yet he possessed a gruff sense of humour and a fondness for a pint which appealed to the broad mass of people. He had, too, a defiant self-confidence in his ability to do the job and get results. That aspect of him was a touch exotic and for a football

> **Journalists gaped as Jack merrily handed out his phone number to the entire press conference.**

Jack's infamous first press conference as Irish manager.

nation that had endured some fifteen years of near misses and bad-luck stories that self-belief was instantly refreshing. Jack was going to touch the parts that other football managers couldn't reach.

His election to the post of Irish manager had been a pleasant shambles which had it occurred in any other country would have seen heads rolling in gutters and careers in tatters. At that time, though, most Irish people trusted the running of Irish football to the FAI in much the same manner as when parking in city centres they leave the protection of their motor cars to elderly beggars in flat caps. Expectations are low but, sure, at least the poor old devils make an effort.

Back in 1986, the poor old devils of the FAI had put their heads together and come up with a cunning plan. Bob Paisley, the most successful manager in English club history, was to be the next Irish manager. The FAI nabobs would be carried through the streets by the populace of a grateful nation.

For media consumption there were officially four candidates for the privilege of succeeding Eoin Hand as Irish manager. Two successful Irish soccer men John Giles and Liam Tuohy. Two imports Jack Charlton and Billy McNeill. Privately the four were to be used as stalking horses. Come the time the great Paisley coup would be unveiled and the former Liverpool manager would become the part-time manager of the Irish national side. A pleasant sinecure in his declining years.

Jack and assistant Maurice Setters before World Cup qualification in Malta, 1989.

On the critical and now celebrated occasion of the FAI's Friday night meeting in February 1986 Paisley's name was duly pulled out of the hat. Billy McNeill's name had been withdrawn from the process at the behest of Manchester City and everything looked like plain sailing. When the eighteen coucil members sat down to vote, though, there was a slight hitch. Canvassing and plotting had indicated that Paisley would get the necessary ten votes on the first ballot. Somebody (speculation on the name is as intense as speculation regarding the Kennedy assassination) changed their mind, however, and Paisley received nine votes. Giles, Tuohy and Charlton picked up three votes each. The FAI took a deep breath and proceeded to a second ballot. Fear and loathing min-

gled with the cigarette smoke down in the bunker. Plots and sub-plots sprang up in paranoid minds. Jack Charlton stomped home as the new Irish manager. Bob Paisley never got the call he was waiting for. Jack, uncontactable at the time, received the glad tidings second-hand from Jimmy Armfield after a game in England.

The following week, the week of his coronation as it were, he gave his first press conference in the Westbury Hotel in Dublin. The usual pleasantries and light snacks were endured by those gathered. Charlton himself was impressive and enthusiastic. Journalists gaped at his innocence as he merrily handed out his home phone number to the entire gathering, not realising that from that moment on his opinion would be ritually canvassed by the media on every issue from football to fishing licences and back.

Towards the end of the press conference the shambolic business of Charlton's election was raised and a question was directed at an FAI member present. In some embarrassment the question was deflected and in the subsequent murmuring Big Jack entered the fray with a crunching tackle. "He," said Charlton, pointing at the embarrassed FAI official, "doesn't have to answer any questions from you."

One voice begged to differ. Well, one voice demanded to differ. That of Eamon Dunphy, a former international footballer who had gone on to enjoy a successful career as an author and polemic journalist. Charlton didn't take well to the first hint of dissent. He cut through the increasingly heated debate by asking Dunphy if he wouldn't rather settle the issue outside. The meaning was clear. Jack Charlton didn't mean that the air-conditioning and acoustics outside would improve the quality of the discourse. He meant that outside was the place to settle the issue so that things inside wouldn't get broken or damaged in the process.

Great centre-halfs in history. Jack with Mick McCarthy, Malta, 1989.

The centre of attention offering his fists to a journalist is not the conventional way of securing column inches and blithely uncritical coverage but Jack Charlton's début in Ireland as a bad-tempered bugger attracted huge attention and ensured that with the exception of Dunphy the Irish media remained cowed and reverential for years afterwards. Almost never in an Irish newspaper is the Irish manager referred to merely by his surname. He is Jack or Big Jack or Our Jack.

It is often assumed by those swooping on the Irish story and finding nothing but romance and blarney that Ireland could scarcely muster a football side in the years before Charlton. For instance, according to one James Dalrymple in the course of a fanciful piece in *The Sunday Times* prior to the World Cup in 1994, the Irish before Charlton were "barely able to raise a team of eleven serviceable pros".

The real problem, however, was one of confidence and organisation. In fact, Ireland's last game before the arrival of Charlton, an uncharacteristically gutless loss to Denmark in the final and for Ireland meaningless game of a World Cup qualifying group, had featured Kevin Moran, Mark Lawrenson, David O'Leary, Jim Beglin, Tony Grealish, Paul McGrath, Liam Brady, Frank Stapleton, Tony Cascarino and Kevin Sheedy, all top-class footballers. Absent that day were regular internationals Gary Waddock and Ronnie Whelan, Chris Hughton and Mick McCarthy. Those players formed the core of Charlton's squad which made it to the European Championships in 1988. What Charlton brought to the task was his simple dogma and his infectious self-confidence. The players he found when he arrived always knew how to kick a football. There were bricks there. Charlton provided the cement.

He has given Irish people pride and a means of expressing it. Also a thread of unity has been provided for those still on the island and the children of the diaspora. Again that dimension of the Irish story has been consistently misunderstood. "The manager and three-quarters of his squad had only marginal Irish connections," wrote Matthew Engel in the *Sports Pages Almanac* of 1991 after Ireland's first appearance in the World Cup finals, "and their football ranged between clodhopping and crass."

Such wilful nonsense, and Engel's contribution wasn't untypical of the genre, has been music to

Jack with Mick Byrne, Noel King and Packie Bonner taking the air at an Irish training session, November 1990.

Jack shows David O'Leary through his paces at Italia '90.

Thoughts of home. Ireland v Italy, quarter-finals, Italia '90.

Irish ears. The crass clodhoppers had drawn with England on a memorable World Cup night in Sardinia. They had beaten the English in Stuttgart in 1988. In March 1991 they would go to Wembley and outplay England once again. Not that beating the English national side hasn't long ago ceased to be a yardstick of progress. The pleasure derives from the irony of English delusions about itself and its relationship with Ireland and the Irish. From the fact that the immense wave of affection and gratitude is directed at an English rogue who never received a reply

when he applied for the English management job.

Early on in his time as Irish manager Jack Charlton acquired the services of John Aldridge and Ray Houghton, both at the time journeymen professionals with Oxford United. Contrary to popular belief, though, he has never sifted through the antecedents of every player in the English league looking for Irish grandparents or evidence of Guinness drinking. Players with Irish connections have tended to gravitate towards the side naturally, or through discussion with other Irish players at club level.

Hughton it was singsongs with his mother's family, the same songs that he would later sing on coaches with his Irish team-mates. Irish players with English accents have been a problem only for the English and for those Irish still pursuing a crabbedly insular and mean spirited version of nationalism.

Through his early years in the Irish job, Charlton's popularity grew phenomenally, from cult to mass worship. Everybody had their Jack Charlton story. He would surprise anglers by wading towards them in the early morning mist to swap information. He arrived unannounced in the unlikeliest of pubs and drunk and sang till closing time. He purchased a house in the west of Ireland. Having professed on his arrival in 1986 that he knew nothing about Ireland he was gracious and open about letting his affection for the place unfold.

As with his playing days and most of his previous management career, his eccentricities and unique appearance endeared him to the broad public. His treatment of several Irish players in the years of his reign has been shoddy and insensitive. Footballers like Liam Brady, Frank Stapleton, Gary Waddock and David O'Leary have all departed the international scene in little clouds of bitterness. As other players join them in growing ranks of the disappeared Charlton's popularity has never even been dented. People can happily accommodate two versions of Jack, however. The great-hearted fisherman and raconteur and the

> **The Charlton technique didn't appear to be tailored so much to the team's talents as the manager's beliefs.**

In remembr-ence of things past. Jack and Franz Becken-baur prior to Ireland's loss to Spain, October 1993.

For Ireland and the Irish, a country ravaged and scarred by centuries of emigration, Irishness isn't merely a factor of the geographical location of one's birth. Irishness is a state of mind, a way of thinking, a cultural inheritance. Irishness is a broad umbrella. In Phil Babb's house it expressed itself maternally through the provision of "God and potatoes". For Andy Townsend it was listening to an aunty from Kerry. For Mick McCarthy it was his father trying to teach him hurling in a Barnsley field. For Ray Houghton it was trips to Parkhead with his Donegal father. For Chris

hardened professional who does what he has to do.

His reign began ignominiously enough. A one-goal defeat to Wales in front of 16,500 mildly curious spectators at Lansdowne Road in March 1986. The Irish players who gathered together that night recall being distinctly unimpressed by what they saw of Charlton that night. The team's physio Mick Byrne was entrusted with picking the team. Big Jack, got out like a country squire, spent most of the evening eyeing up his new charges. There were intense reservations and a little confusion about the proposed style of play. Midfield, which housed the genius of Brady, was prohibited from accepting passes from the defence. Instead midfield was to hare forward and support the front players who were coping with an endless supply of long balls.

Charlie O'Leary, Irish kitman, discusses the odds with the Pope, while Jack and company look on.

Midfield play had long been the great pride of the Irish team and support. In the days when both Giles and Brady ran that particular show together there was a popular joke about the Irish midfield which had to be performed in the voice of any well-known commentator. "Giles looking for the crossfield ball, beautiful, and Brady takes possession from Giles, moving into space wide on the right, pauses, looks up, plays the pass to Stapleton, Stapleton beats one, beats another, rounds the goalkeeper, he's through, Stapleton has to score, oh yes and played safely back by Stapleton to Giles in midfield. Giles looks for Brady..."

The new Charlton technique didn't appear to be tailored so much to the team's talents as the manager's beliefs. However, when the side went to Iceland in the summer of 1986 and won an inconsequential triangular tournament and the first piece of silverware the side had ever won, necessitating the purchase of a modest trophy cabinet, sufficient numbers were swayed.

That trip established Charlton's authority within the squad. The unfortunate victim of that process being David O'Leary, who having been omitted from Jack's plans for the tour, booked a family holiday only to be ordered to get his bag and boots by the new Irish manager, who found

Taking the laurels after Ireland's heroic exit to Italy, Rome 1990.

69

himself in the middle of an injury crisis with the trip imminent. O'Leary declined to cancel his arrangements for the sake of a couple of off-season friendlies. For his impudence he suffered several years in lonely exile. Even when O'Leary rehabilitated himself sufficiently to merit inclusion in the panel for the 1990 World Cup finals, going on to score the vital goal which brought Ireland to the quarter-finals, a frosty distance always existed between himself and Jack Charlton.

The Icelandic sortie also marked a new and welcome phase of Jack's professional development. The Irish set-up differed in many obvious respects from that which Jack had encountered at club management level. Irish players were accustomed to freely socialising with their manager. Over the years of defeats and near misses the group had evolved into a knot of tight friendships and interdependencies. Charlton's easy manner and natural garrulousness earned him admission to the group. On discovering that Iceland was a country bereft of pubs or off-licences Charlton had purchased extravagant amounts of beer for the squad at the airport. He also displayed a willingness to stand up and cut the air with a song when the occasion demanded it.

Jack's singing was always heartfelt. To stand up and sing a song to a group of virtual strangers is a difficult business which strips a person of many protective layers. Charlton would sometimes be drawn to tears after singing an old English ballad or giving out his new favourite "Dublin in the Rare Oul Times". After several years on the chicken-dinner-and-chat-show circuit as a middle-of-the-

Jack trades jokes in training before the Ireland v Poland European qualifier in 1991.

range celebrity Jack appeared to be discovering new aspects of his own personality and being.

Qualification for the European Championships of 1988 came as an unexpected bonus. With Ireland's qualifying programme finished, progress to the finals in Germany depended on Scotland beating Bulgaria away from home. As Bulgaria hadn't been beaten at home since seeds were planted in the garden of Eden and since Scotland had no incentive to win and Bulgaria only needed a draw for qualification the European Championships were written off as yet another hard-luck tale. New manager, same old story.

Gary Mackay is the most enigmatic of all Irish heroes. In Sofia he scored the eighty-seventh-minute goal for Scotland on 11 November 1987 which slipped Ireland through to the finals of a

major football competition for the first time in history. Loved and revered though Gary Mackay is in Ireland he could slip through any gathering there totally unrecognised.

Jack Charlton has always been a charmed man. Life is good to him. On his first attempt he had brought an international side to a major tournament. Qualification was merited but so many Irish had lost out due to freakish goals like Gary Mackay's in the past, that it was hard to accept that Jack wasn't in some way kissed by the gods.

The initial foray into the big time, the European Championships of 1988 set the tone for the Charlton style. In the weeks leading up to the players' departure for Germany the surly demeanour which radiates from most international football squads was absent from the Irish. Ireland weren't about to hear "The Executioner's Song" if they came home without a win. Being in Germany was a triumph. The nation would be content if humiliation was avoided. Ten days before the team departed training was interrupted in order that the squad might enjoy a day at the races. Jack, charmed man, won on every race. The day at the races dissolved into a night at the pub and a morning in bed.

Charlton discusses tactics with Irish captain Andy Townsend before the Ireland v Poland game, 1991.

Ireland's presence transformed the clinical, antiseptic nature of the European Championships into something beerier and more soulful. Some 15,000 to 20,000 Irish fans swamped Germany with song and celebration. In one of those uniquely emotional Irish hours, England were beaten in the first game of the competition. Ray Houghton's unlikely looping header which fooled Peter Shilton in the fifth minute was virtually the last time the Irish threatened the English goal.

For eighty-five minutes Ireland improvised a furious, crazed, rearguard action. At the long whistle there were tears and delirium. That win over Charlton's own nation meant so much to Ireland and the Irish. In London in the following days emigrants began scribbling the modest legend 1-0 on the walls of the underground, the score-line serving as a silent code to others scraping

Jack rages after three-all draw with Poland, October 1991.

away in an alien culture. "I hope England go through as well," said Charlton in the aftermath. "I'm still an Englishman, you know." The nation knew that, but was graciously willing to overlook the fact.

Following a draw with the USSR the competition ended for Ireland when a freakishly spinning ball bounced off a Dutch head on to the turf, taking an unlikely trajectory into the back of Bonner's net. Nobody cared much. The experience was summed up in a pat but philosophical formula – England: won, should have lost; USSR: drew, should have won; Holland: lost, should have drawn. Whatever way it was added up it amounted to three points and a trip home.

Charlton's eccentric will and personality had become a corner-stone of the success. Ball-players like Liam Brady, who missed the tournament due to a three-game suspension, had bowed to the Charlton way. His running and toiling was thoroughbred workhorse style and his class eventually began to shine through again. There were minor miracles, too. Before the Dutch game injury worries had mounted. Charlton made them disappear by force of will. Packie Bonner incurred a serious back strain in the course of the Russian game

Batman and Robin. Jack and Maurice Setters, Spain 1991.

which restricted his movements and effectively ruled him out of the game with Holland. Twenty-four hours beforehand the big goalie shuffled off to give the news to Jack. Bonner danced about the subject for a little while in Jack's room and then laid it on the line. Couldn't move. Professional thing to do. Fairness to other players. Fairness to fans. "If you don't play," said Jack, "you'll be letting me down. Now get on with it." Next day Packie played. When he returned home to Ireland a brief medical exploration revealed a damaged disc in his back.

From the time of the European Championships onwards, from the instant of the final whistle in the English game, Jack Charl-

ton became an industry and a cult in Ireland. Those who cavilled privately about the new Irish way of playing football being ugly ran the risk of being deported. Everything was coming up beautiful. The rampant Irish forward line would run up an impressive one-goal tally in four games as the squad began to steam through the World Cup qualifying campaign later in 1988. Charlton's confidence buoyed up the nation. This guy was a winner. Trips to Italy in 1990 were being booked long before Jack Charlton's team knew for certain that they would be travelling.

That summer of Ireland's first World Cup campaign may have changed the national character for ever. These massive, wonderfully inclusive footballing celebrations were becoming a part of the national fabric. Jack became a beaming master of ceremonies as Ireland swooned and swaggered at his feet. The open-heartedness of it all moved him. When it finally came time to leave, when the team had bowed out at the end of an indelible night against the Italians in Rome, it was Charlton who dallied longest walking around the Olympic Stadium bleary-eyed, grasping a tricolour in one hand and a drink in the other, waving and grinning to those who had travelled with him for the previous few weeks. He said afterwards that he had been able to smell the final that night, that his disappointment in defeat was intense but the swell of emotion and support from the stands swept him along, moved him deeply. It was Jack who was last on to the plane home at Leonardo da Vinci airport. Big Jack was drinking in every last drop of this World Cup. Ireland was proud of him and he was proud of Ireland. The worshipped and the worshippers bowed to each other.

He has reflected since that the Italia '90 experience was unique. Back in 1966 Jack won the first World Cup he participated in and went home to Yorkshire the following day. The magic of the communal celebration washed over him. What he had achieved was a professional goal. Everything was strictly internalised. Afterwards at other World Cups working as an analyst for ITV the crew would use Jack's well-known face as an accreditation to get them into training grounds where other crews never trespassed. "Hey, Jack, whistle to Dino Zoff and get him over." The great brotherhood of football unlocked many doors and gates for the big man. During the course of those tournaments he hankered after life on the training ground.

Second thoughts. Charlton watches Ireland beat Holland at Tilberg during the build-up to World Cup 1994.

"I used to wonder what it would be like to be there with me own team. I was there with the telly but it wasn't the same thing. You are locked out. I wanted to be at the centre of it again, to appreciate it all."

Again the exodus from Ireland was heavy and haphazard. The tales of life on the lam in Italy have been absorbed into the national folklore. There are the groups which travelled overland from London in poorly air-conditioned vans. There are those who made the trip out to Sardinia for the English match in a catamaran, a craft which encountered some difficulties along the way. There was the moving televisual moment when Ireland finally beat the Romanians on penalties when a camera homed in on the face of the renowned Irish political journalist John Healy. For years Healy had been an incorrigible thorn in the side of authority, pugnaciously landing punches on the left, the right and the cowardly centre. As David O' Leary stroked his penalty to the net and Ireland advanced to the quarter-finals Healy, standing in a crowded and largely hysterical roomful of people watching events unfold on a big screen, began to cry. Large slow tears ran down his great Irish face. Peo-

ple watched John Healy cry and they cried too.

It was that kind of month. There was the tale of the photojournalist who burned his genitals while experimenting with flaming sambucas in a restuarant one night. Through the whole anthology runs the theme of adventure and journeying, the peripatetic Irish fans jaunting around Italy in a great delirious caravan of green and gold.

There were foot-balling tales, too, small slices of sporting soap opera which brought the team and manager down to human dimen-sions. David O' Leary re-called at long last to the fold scored the penalty in the shoot-out with Romania which put Ireland into the quarter-finals of their first World Cup. He was buried under a great green mound of celebrating foot-ballers, all sins forgotten. Gary Waddock, the pop-ular and fiery midfielder, had been a surprise inclusion in Charlton's initial travelling party

"You'll never beat the Irish, you'll never beat the Irish."

which left for pre-tournament preparation in Malta on 25 May. Waddock played poorly in a friendly with Turkey, however, while two days later Ray Houghton reported that he was suffering a pelvic strain which threatened his participation. Charlton needed to summon a new attacking midfielder before he named his squad for FIFA. Waddock was sent home and Alan McLoughlin was summoned to Malta. The heart ached for Waddock, who had heroically fought back from long-term injury to become part of the squad. Charlton declines to discuss the incident these days, dismissing it as "just another decision a manager must make", but at the time his sense of guilt and regret was immense and heightened further when it was revealed that upon returning Waddock had declined a large cash offer from a Sunday tabloid to tell his story in newsprint.

It didn't seem possible but Jack's popularity broke through to another dimension that summer. The opening game with England in Sardinia brought fears that Bobby Robson's side might exact retribution for their humiliation in Stuttgart twenty-four months earlier. England scored early, when Gary Lineker punished a sequence of sloppy

play in the Irish defence. The long-feared skinning of Mick McCarthy was about to begin, perhaps. Ireland fought back, however, fingernails scratching on the precipice. A goal from Kevin Sheedy secured a draw. All around Cagliari the eerie dirge sounded: "You'll never beat the Irish, you'll never beat the Irish." Players and fans celebrated deep into the night. Finally Jack rounding up his squad had to threaten disciplinary action on several players who were disinclined to turn in for the night without the company of their wives. As usual Charlton had his way and apologies were forthcoming in the morning.

The difficulties of living for some seven weeks with the pampered professionals of the English league are perhaps the sole drawback Charlton encounters on these idyllic footballing trips. Throughout the Italian tournament his refusal to give Ronnie Whelan playing time of more than twenty minutes as a sub was a constant bone of contention. Whelan, at the high point of a splendid career with Liverpool, bridled and argued his case consistently. Whelan and Charlton had heated rows both before the tournament in Malta and afterwards in Italy. Whelan repeatedly told

Jack argues the toss with referee and linesman in the World Cup qualifier against Lithuania, Vilnius, 1993.

Before the deluge. Jack in training prior to the October 1993 loss to Spain.

Big Times manager Jack Charlton at European Championships in Germany, 1988.

Charlton through reporters and their newspapers that he was fit to play, a method of communication which Charlton despised. The feud continued all the way back to Ireland with Whelan waving a copy of the Sunday newspaper at Charlton on the flight home angrily urging Charlton to read the testimony of others.

The soccer wars only served to heighten Jack's popularity at home. The broad mass of people instinctively backed him in his troubles. When things got down to *mano a mano* scrapping with Eamon Dunphy after Ireland's disappointing performance against Egypt, what debate there had been about Charlton became rapidly polarised. You backed Charlton or you backed Dunphy. The middle ground was just for casualties. The nation by and large backed Charlton.

Dunphy, working as a television analyst for RTE, became enraged at the prosaic nature of an unambitious and drab Irish performance against the Egyptians on a warm Italian Sunday afternoon. Eamon's bonnet is seldom free of bees and on this occasion he vented his considerable spleen by flinging his biro across a television studio and announcing that this was an Irish performance to be ashamed of. This simple comment became distorted as it winged its way around Italy later that evening and people swore that Dunphy had said that he was ashamed to be Irish. What might have been an interesting debate about the Irish side's ambition and penetration lurched instead towards being a personal duel which Jack Charlton couldn't lose.

When at last the odyssey ended, and the side returned home, Charlton was surprised and mildly embarrassed to find half a million people lining the streets to welcome himself and his team home. "We have won nothing," he told the sea of people. He was wrong. Ireland had won far more than silverware or medals. Soccer is the great world game, the one language which is truly universal. Two point four billion people had watched some part of the World Cup finals. Ireland had been an integral part of that great glory. Jack Charlton, an Englishman, had granted that gift.

CHAPTER FIVE

BACK IN THE USA

Charlton grew into the job of Irish manager, his prickly person changing into a somewhat quixotic figure tilting vainly at the windmills of footballing bureaucracy. As FIFA discovered at the US World Cup, Jack Charlton had never learned how to bow or curtsy.

(Previous pages) With Irish caption Andy Townsend at Seminole County training ground, 1994.

One World Cup night in the Hilton Hotel in Orlando while Jack Charlton and his team slept the sleep of the blessed up on the eighth floor a group of journalists and supporters argued the odds in the lobby. It was the eve of the Dutch game and confidence was running high.

There were as many different opinions of Charlton as there were people gathered at the table. He strikes me as a mean man, said one. A list of generous Charlton deeds was solemnly enunciated by others in the group. Somebody ventured that the Charlton demeanour was one of ignorance, not a man to read a book. On a flight from New York to Washington, however, somebody had seen Charlton's nose deep in a history of the Reevers and other border peoples. Every deed of Charltonesque insensitivity was trumped with a tale of Charlton grace. His moments of bullying with the press were counterpointed with the fact that often in the evenings he would seek out the company of senior journalists for meals and drinks. Up on the eighth floor a great enigma was slumbering.

Eamon Dunphy was in irrepressible mood that night, argumentative and lively, his mind jumping

Another day, another press conference – Jack and friends, Orlando 1994.

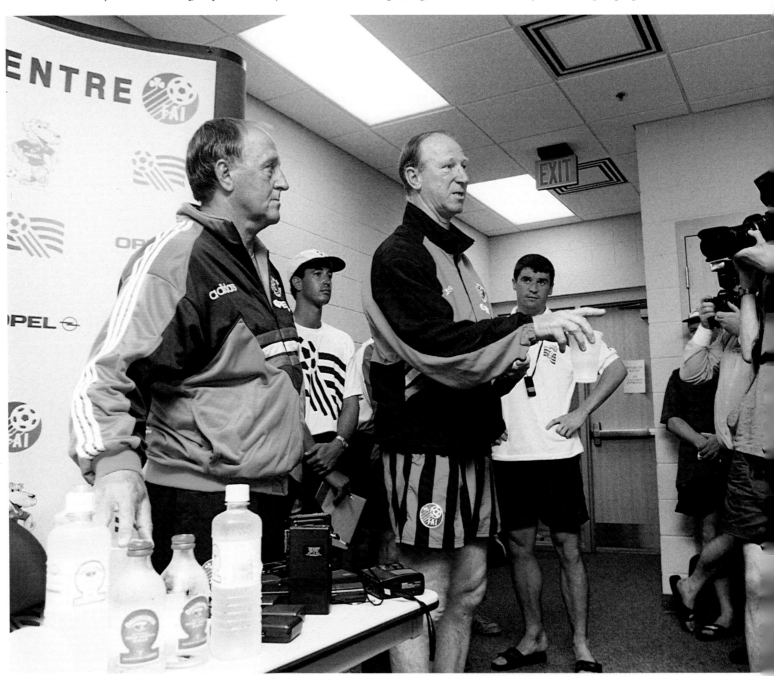

from topic to topic with such strange alacrity that the gathering gave up arguing and settled down to watch instead. It didn't take long before he hit upon a favourite and compelling theme. How the Charlton style had infected Irish football. How the hoofing game was a betrayal of all the great Irish footballers who had toiled and struggled before Ireland reached the land of milk and honey.

In many ways Eamon Dunphy is right. As Jack's own team has grown and evolved into a competent and combative passing unit the legacy of these great years is the disturbing sight of Irish under-age teams hacking the ball aimlessly and endlessly towards gangly centre forwards off whom the ball caroms like a pinball. If there has been a betrayal of traditions, though, it hasn't been Charlton who has perpetrated it. The betrayal has been a communal one.

Jack Charlton has come to Ireland and done his job, done that which he was hired to do. The spin-offs have been enormous. Three times the real world has been suspended as Ireland transfixes itself on a soccer tournament in some part of the globe. Charlton himself has turned into a major industry, earning it is alleged some £500,000 a year through endorsement deals. He draws an income, too, through his relationship with various newspapers and his wage from the FAI. He has kept his part of the bargain. If the memory of great but unfulfilled players in the Irish pantheon hasn't been sufficiently honoured, if the Irish genius for creativity hasn't been given full expression it is because the nation was more than willing to swap gleaming moments and defeat for sturdiness and full-blown success.

In truth the football story of the last eight years is relatively dull. A good bunch of international-grade professionals have through organisation and spirit begun qualifying for major tournaments. What is more remarkable is the cultural turmoil which has gone along with that modest achievement. Ireland is a great and truly sporting nation, which has never taken balance sheets and national debts seriously enough to allow them to detract from the enjoyment of a sporting spectacle. Where economics exists as a force in Irish life it exists in the micro, in the life of the individual. It exists in terms of jobs lost and children emigrated and taxes stoically offered up. It is all borne with a gentle courage and heroism and the deeds of the football team over the eight years or so of Charlton's management have lightened the load.

If there is a betrayal of the country's professional football past it has been made eagerly and desperately. Those names that were wreathed with glory in the past provided themselves with an escape from the grime of our cities and they provided those that watched them with the chance to dream. In a great and inflated way that process has continued. If the football is different, and the need to win a little more pressing, then there is no doubt that Rosie Henderson and Charlie Hurley and Kit Lawlor and Bunny Fulham and the whole pantheon will understand.

And the need to win is certainly becoming more pressing. Before he left for America on 6 June Jack was a long string of stresses and tensions. He was worried about the heat. "We come from Ireland, not the bloody Gobi desert." He was fretting about the English tabloids. "One of them steps out of line and I'll sue. I have the money and I'll do it." He was anxious about tactics and selection. "If I don't play with the young lads and things go wrong I'll be to blame. If I play them and things go wrong, I'll be to blame. They don't know our system well enough but they can play a bit. I don't know just yet."

'The fish was this big, I tell you.' Jack in Orlando, 1994.

In the heat of Orlando alone with his players at last he relaxed a little. The morning trips to Seminole County training centre became a pleasant routine. The team black-shirted and competitive would be put through their paces while Jack wandered through the proceedings, pegging the odd ball at an empty net, taking injury-niggled players aside for a quiet word and occasionally bawling out some poor victim who wasn't doing things the Charlton way.

The press conferences that followed each session had a relaxed feel to them. American journal-

ists coming to the story of the Irish soccer team eight years later than the rest of the world daily risked the wrath of Charlton by asking him to plod back over the whole tale. "What have you done for Irish soccer, Mr Charlton, and why did you take this job?" Typically, a long baleful glare would freeze the questioner's blood. "Ah. I'm tired of being asked that. Ask one of these Irish lads afterwards." And the moment would subside.

The tension bubbled up volcanically on occasion though. One warm afternoon the squad decided upon a lengthy session which if they survived it would get them over the acclimatisation hump. Everyone pushed each other on, everyone feeling free to have a go at any player who was slacking or slipping in the soupy humidity. In the no-holds-barred atmosphere which was to get everyone through the session several harsh words of encouragement wafted through the still air to the press contingent, who took no notice. One tabloid however, a paper which takes any type of ink, felt there might be a good "row" story to be had out of a briefly overheard exchange between Roy Keane and assistant manager Maurice Setters. Another journalist, an entirely innocent party in the whole affair, approached Charlton's press agent to check if there was any truth in this rumour. Angry editors phoning hotel rooms first thing in the morning need to know that certain rival scoops are, well, artificially enhanced. This simple journalistic enquiry got back to Charlton as evidence that Irish newspapers intended running a row story the following morning. Setters and Keane were marched in before the press corps. Jack performed the briefest of interrogations. "Maurice, did you have a row with Roy?" "No, boss." "Roy, did you have a row with Maurice?" "No, boss." "Now there you are. I don't like it when you people try to undermine us."

Those accustomed to Jack's methods merely scribbled down their accounts of the proceedings and thanked the heavens for a good colour story which would break the monotony. The American media folk were astounded. This Jack Charlton guy was a story unto himself.

Charlton is to this day perplexed and confused about where things began going wrong for the team.

What Jack despises most is the waiting, the long finger-drumming months, days and hours when the media get on his case with their idle speculation and the permutations play havoc with his brain. This had been a long, long wait. Ireland had qualified for the US World Cup on a stormy, tension-soaked night back in Belfast in November 1983. Having lost to Spain the previous month Ireland not so much breasted the tape but stumbled across it that night. Ireland through an unlikely goal from Alan McLoughlin had secured a draw while simultaneously in Seville ten Spaniards were beating Denmark, a result which saw Ireland through to the US on goal difference. Jack's charm had worked again. The heart and soul of Jack's ageing team had outlasted the body. He had scraped the last out of his heroically dogged squad.

Happenstance decreed that the Northern Irish match was played in the bloody wash of some of the worst sectarian violence the north had seen in recent decades. Played out in a siege atmosphere amidst the seething hatreds of a frightened city those ninety minutes required ordinary footballers, young men whose breadth of experience matches the breadth of the biggest dressing room they have been in, to dig deep into their reserves of courage and bravery. The support which had trudged with the team from Copenhagen to Tirana to Seville and through the Baltics was barred from Belfast for the final lap. It was easy to be lonely and scared with a southern accent at Windsor Park that night.

Alan Kernaghan, a son of Belfast, played centre-back for Ireland that night, and was shaken by

Hat, shades, attitude, US 1994

the acidic bile hurled his way. "Lundy" and "Fenian scum" he could cope with. The references and bristling threats to his parents upset him. Afterwards in the dressing room when all eyes were shining and focused on America Kernaghan dissolved into tears. Phil Babb remembers that night, too, remembers gazing in horror out the window of the team coach on the way to Windsor Park and seeing a ten-year-old drop his football and crumple his right hand into the shape of a gun which he fired, one eye shut for aim, at Babb. Paul McGrath and Terry Phelan, the two

black Irishmen on the field that night, felt the stinging cocktail of racism and sectarianism every time they touched the ball. Kevin Moran, out of action through injury, took his seat in the stand while a forest of Union Jack tatooed fists waved at him. In the end they survived. Isolated as never before from their green-flagged supporters and hangers-on the side had little to draw upon but their own resources.

Watching the team train, however, beneath the smog-softened lights of Windsor Park on the eve of the match it was curious and striking how a life in

professional football insulates and protects young minds. Playing a brief practice game across the width of a pitch with corner flags serving as goals the professional footballers of Ireland were imagining nothing other than life as professional footballers. When they scored they threw their arms aloft and hugged as if they had never experienced such a novelty before. As they dribbled and ran and passed they supplied their own Motson-inflected commentaries and crowd noises: "Just wide but gets an appreciating ooooh from the crowd, Townsend feeds Aldo, Aldo is through, the plonker must score...yeeheeeess!!!" That sense of preserved childhood makes life as a footballer interesting and tolerant to grown men. It got the team through two days of ugliness in November also.

Afterwards the team and officials and attendant media retinue fled from the grimy city and its dark skies before midnight to be welcomed home in the wee hours by jubilant throngs at Dublin airport. "We're on the one road," sang the team before disembarking on home soil again. It was half true. Some of the heroes who had brought Ireland to America weren't going to play there.

That was Jack's great headache. The game in Belfast had revealed the first signs that Jack's breezy confidence was failing. During the game he became strangely involved in an unpleasant exchange with the Northern Ireland bench. When Northern Ireland scored early in the second half by means of a stunning piece of creativity wholly out of place in a game of such passionate sterility, Jack became conscious of a virulent wave of abuse being directed at him from the Northern Irish bench. When Alan McLoughlin drove home the equaliser Jack felt the urge to reciprocate and did so imaginatively.

Lights, camera, action. Jack trades sharp words with Billy Bingham, November 1993.

Afterwards when feelings normally dissolve

Charlton had a verbal cut at Northern Irish manager Billy Bingham. To his shame Bingham had stoked the menace of the crowd all week, driving the temperature on the night past that which was tolerable by waving his arms in encouragement to the terraces. Instantly, though, Jack regretted his outburst and with his usual sense of tact and drama he burst into Bingham's press conference to deliver a gruff and sincere apology.

Charlton is to this day perplexed and confused about where things began going wrong for the team. As a player he played on until he was thirty eight years old and he doesn't subscribe wholeheartedly therefore to the theory that too many legs began creaking at the same time. If he has to put his finger on it he blames his half-time talk during the third last qualifying game in September 1993 against Lithuania. After seven years of unremitting positivism in the dressing room, after over seventy games when he simply urged his players to go for it, Charlton told his team to take the foot off the pedal for the second half. The spectre of the Spanish visiting Lansdowne Road the following month was on his mind, several players were carrying yellow-card offences which could in the heat of battle develop into full-blown

Shirt, tie, more attitude.

With Taoiseach Albert Reynolds (left) and Tanaiste Dick Spring (right) at Dublin airport, July 1994.

fined by FIFA for reasons which were never adequately explained. The great and pompous men of FIFA don't take kindly to pricklish, independent folk like Jack Charlton who don't know when to bow or how to curtsy.

Right through the tournament Charlton itched to lock horns with the tedious bureaucrats and rule slaves who were running the competition. On the day before Ireland opened their programme, Jack's press conference in Giants Stadium descended into farce as a blazered official decided that Jack couldn't speak unless his agent was present beside him. Charlton amazed and in a hurry proceeded to take questions. The blazered one kept hectoring Charlton, "Stop, stop." Eventually Charlton's agent John Givens ambled by and was collared by the fuming blazer. While Charlton discussed his team an intriguing sideshow of a row developed with Givens filling The Blazer in on some facts of life about dealing with Jack Charlton. Eventually somebody roared, "Shut up!" Jack took the opportunity to make a bad-tempered escape.

On the playing front the crisis regarding the lack of a quality forward remained but other problems had solved themselves. Some of the old luck recrudesced when three young players of outstanding quality blossomed before Jack's eyes in the preamble to the World Cup. Gary Kelly, Phil Babb and Jason McAteer all grew to international stature in a freakishly short length of time. If Jack had been on a truly hot streak, though, a thirty-goal-a-season forward would have sprung from the heavens with Irish qualifications and the touch of a genius. What he got instead was Tommy Coyne, a bright but paceless forward with Motherwell, a man who was still recovering from the death the previous summer of his young wife. Tommy Coyne wasn't too much pushed about football at the time but he was the best bet available as America loomed.

With Quinn laid low, and Aldridge no longer possessing the change of pace that once bought him prairies of space and with Cascarino struggling for fitness all season, scoring goals was always

suspensions. So with a two-goal lead in the bag he told them to ease up.

There is no reason to suppose that players instructed to ease up in the second half of a game in September will still be struggling to shake off their lethargy a month later, but some part of Jack Charlton believes that he broke a spell at half-time that day against Lithuania. Whatever happened, he had six months of headaches facing him before the team left for the States.

Suddenly life wasn't a steady hail of blessings for the Irish any more. In November Big Niall Quinn trundled over a booby-trapped tuft of grass and tore the ligaments in his knee ruling him out of the World Cup. In December when the World Cup draw was made Ireland were sent not to Boston as had been pleasurably anticipated but to Orlando and New York. Worse was the company the team were to keep: Norway, Mexico, Italy. Two World Cups and Ireland had found their way into the so-called Group of Death both times. Charlton smiled the smile of the Grim Reaper and heaped further troubles on his own head by declining to go to a managers' workshop conference in New York in February.

FIFA couldn't keep Jack back after school or give him extra homework for his non-attendance but they could remember the fact of it. Four years earlier Jack had declined to attend the managers' workshop prior to the Italian World Cup. During that tournament he had to be reprimanded by FIFA for his behaviour on the touch-line during the Romanian game. During USA '94 he was

Charlton's great strength as a manager has always been his ability to cocoon his players from pressure.

going to be a problem in the States. Come spring, Jack looked at his resources, an abundance of midfielders, various uncertainties hovering over Alan Kernaghan and Paul McGrath in the middle of defence, Smart Boy Wanted sign in the window up front. Jack opted to play 4-5-1. Finding the one would be a problem. He didn't enjoy the departure this represented from the great certainties and simple beliefs which had governed his football life for over forty years but there was little he could do. Five midfielders? The time for fannying on had arrived.

When Ireland finally got into a World Cup dressing room, somewhere in the bowels of Giants Stadium with the songs of 60,000 Irish outside nothing but a muffled distraction, all Jack's thinking had been done. He would play football against the Italians that afternoon. He would match them

pass for pass and wile for wile and the hard-work ethic that had been bred into his own players would compensate for any gulf in technique between the two sides. Tommy Coyne would start up front. John Sheridan, a player about whom Charlton had long held suspicions, would be the play-maker in midfield. Phil Babb, a cultured young centre-half not much given to hoofing, would partner McGrath at the centre of defence.

Everything progressed beautifully until the team strode out into the tunnel wearing as instructed their white jerseys. The Italians were in white also. Charlton's great strength as a manager has always been his ability to cocoon his players from pressure. In the minutes before the team had left the dressing room he had been quiet and collected. Players tapped footballs to each other while Charlton told them that being here was an

Lost cause. Ireland go down 2-1 against Mexico in Orlando, 1994.

achievement, that the pressure was off, that World Cups were for enjoyment and fulfilment. Suddenly with the realisation that the team shirts had to be changed, the levee broke. It broke all over kitman Charlie O'Leary. "Whatcha mean, Chulie, that we're in the wrong shirts? Whatcha fookin' mean?" Long gangly Charlton's almost

comical rage with five-foot Charlie achieved what all the calm, calm words hadn't. The tension rushed out through the valve of laughter.

Afterwards when Ray Houghton's goal had secured a victory that for merit and pleasure equalled anything in the nation's history, Jack Charlton went out on to the fresh turf of Giants

to the pitch. The local constabulary had reacted as if that silly exuberant trespass represented a plot to undermine the entire American way of life. Jack incensed by what he saw remonstrated angrily with the police as the fans were led away. For moments of decency like that Jack Charlton earns the right to be forgiven anything.

Fans. They had been one of the wonders of the afternoon. From an allocation of 3,500 tickets some 60,000 Irish had managed to infiltrate the stadium. The immense cookie cutter structure was festooned with green, white and gold and the thick New Jersey air boiled with song. When finally Jack came off the pitch, into the three-quarters darkness of the tunnel which circulates beneath the stadium, all that was visible of him for one brief instant was the glowing of his cigar, a cigar as big as a zeppelin. The waiting journalists hushed, expecting to hear the familiar strains of "Air on the G string."

He disappeared into the throbbing heart of the dressing room where his great long frame was crushed again and again in the arms of his players. Mick Byrne, the team physio, was in tears. Ray Houghton was jubilant. Charlton had goaded him to extraordinary effort on the training fields of Seminole County with a stinging series of public pronouncements concerning Houghton's decline as a player. Houghton's presence and ability to perform on the big day had always been an emblem of the Charlton era. Houghton had made his début on the same night as Charlton took up his duties as boss. He had played in fifty-eight of the subsequent seventy-eight games, only injury, suspension and the occasional need to experiment costing him his place in the other twenty games. Ireland's only two victories in major competition had been the products of Houghton goals. Charlton and Houghton hugged each other doubtfully. Two serious football men still proving things to each other.

Charlton emerged once more into the half-gloom of the media interview zone and took receipt of a crushing embrace from the Taoiseach, Albert Reynolds. No amount of EU hand-outs

Sustenance. Charlton keeps Steve Staunton fuelled during the World Cup game against Norway in Giants Stadium, New Jersey, 1994.

Jack was infected by an incurable anxiety about the heat in Orlando.

Stadium to be with the crowd. Earlier he had endeared himself to them once again, looking after a couple of their number at a time when his mind could forgivably have been on other things. When the final whistle had blown late but welcome two Irish fans overcome with the need to touch the hems of players' garments had leapt on could buy this transfusion of the national morale. It became a politician to be grateful to a sportsman.

Next day Charlton was businesslike and brusque as usual. His players had flown back to base in Orlando the previous night. Charlton had work to do, however, shuttling on to Washington to study the form of the other group teams Mexico and Norway.

Since the draw for the finals had been made Jack had been infected by an incurable anxiety about the heat in Orlando. FIFA have long since ceased worrying about the World Cup being a process to ascertain the best football team in the world. For some years the powers that be have submitted the World Cup competition to serfdom under the rule of television. The World Cup must be a flowing, all-singing, all-dancing prime-time

At the Seminole Training centre in Orlando, 1994.

spectacle whatever the cost. If that means playing under the noonday sun in Orlando, so be it.

In the aftermath of the Italian carnival in New Jersey Tommy Coyne had been a very sick man, coming to the verge of collapse with nausea and headaches induced by dehydration. The sight of Coyne, pale, weak and sick fed Charlton's alarm. Jack spent the week railing against FIFA and fretting about the heat. It was his nature, but it scarcely helped. The team went into that Friday game with Mexico in a messy state mentally. There was the gnawing thought that a draw would probably be sufficient to ensure a place in the second round. There was the hang-up about the heat. Then there was the practical joke played by the weather which cooled all week long only to rise to a humidity-laden 120 degrees on match day.

Ireland's performance against Mexico was inhibited and sluggish. Several players were unduly worried and affected by the heat. Steve Staunton had taken to wearing a hat in the pre-match kick around, hardly the sign of a healthy psyche dealing with the problem. Repeatedly balls from defence were played long and hurried down the park. The Mexicans hussled in much the manner that Ireland had patented. By half-time it was 2-0.

The second half unravelled differently. There is a theory about football in the heat which puts forward the notion that the only way to cope is to play one's way into the game. The more a player worries about heat the more it will inhibit him. In the second half with their backs to the wall and with a blast from Charlton to remind them what real heat was the Irish rallied, enjoying possession aplenty. A celebrated scene unfolded on the touch-line as John Aldridge sought to enter the fray as a substitute while the FIFA representative mulled over the paperwork. The word "Dickhead" was heard in American living rooms for possibly the first time. Aldridge gained admission to the game eventually and scored a goal, in the dying minutes.

They left it at that, 2-1. Afterwards in the cool of the dressing room the humdrum business of dressing and showering and avoiding each other's eyes was rudely interrupted. Charlton gathered his players in a big circle and spoke intently for ten minutes. The World Cup was a struggle now. Italy was history. Defeat to Norway would mean a plane home and ignominy. The plans for a weekend of gentle leisure and a visit to DisneyWorld were scrapped. Players voted to train in New Jersey as soon as they arrived there on Sunday evening. Out of defeat Charlton had formulated a plan. Players had a focus again. They left to face the media. Out on the podium talking to the press, Jack's fuse ran short

'Actually, the fish was this big.' Jack passes the time on a rainy day in Florida.

once more. Mexicans had evidently been wounded by Charlton's assertion that theirs was a very hot country. Mexican journalists goaded Charlton about his complaints over the heat. "We'll play you on a nice wet winter's day sometime, like what we're used to," said Jack, trying to make the issue vanish with a joke. But the Mexicans persisted. "It wasn't very hot when Mexico played Ireland in 1984 and you didn't win that game either, Mr Charlton." Silence. There was a mild detonation on the stage and Jack announced he'd had enough of the Mexican media, they could write about their own team for tomorrow. He, Jack, was going to talk to the Irish. He stalked down off the platform and straight into the knot of Irish journalists. FIFA folk in blazers screamed nervily into their walkie-talkies. "We've got a non-control situation in the mixed zone. Repeat. Non-control situation." Back in the team hotel there was almost another non-control situation. A group of journalists milled about Charlton looking for his explanations and thoughts. Eamon Dunphy put a question to Jack regarding the tactics deployed that afternoon. Jack examined the ceiling and studied the floor. Finally he gave his verdict. "Not going to win no fooking World Cup in this heat." Dunphy in an apparent sea change had been touting Ireland as true contenders for the trophy on account of some startling results in friendlies leading up to the tournament.

George Best once alleged that Jack Charlton backed out on the Newcastle United job because he lacked the bottle necessary to tackle the job. Neither Jack nor Bobby Charlton would ever have found themselves to have much in common with Best, who was the antithesis to everything imparted in the finishing schools of Ashington, Northumberland. The point is an interesting one, though. Jack does many things very well as a manager, but handling pressure isn't one of them.

When he wants to be he is a superb handler and motivator of players. His treatment of Paul McGrath and his numerous problems over the years has been masterfully subtle. Jack has wrung the very best out of the wayward genius. As regards reading a football game Jack is peerless.

As the World Cup rolled on, however, Best's bottle question began to nag a little. Jack was becoming increasingly irritable. The team returned to New York and played well in securing a goalless draw with Norway, a result which bought the Irish admission into the second round and, it seemed, a clash with Belgium back in Orlando. The prospect of returning to Orlando was immediately deemed to be the cloud around the silver lining.

Next day, Jack took off for Washington in

Final words. Charlton's press conference upon home-coming after the 1994 World Cup.

order to study the Belgians in action against the Saudi Arabians. Rather disobligingly the Belgians lost and on the merest whisker of goal difference Holland transpired to be Ireland 's second-round opponents. Disgruntled at having made a wasted trip Jack made his way to the airport to find a connection to Orlando. There weren't any till morning. He phoned several hotels. No room at the inns. Somebody advised him that if he flew to Atlanta, which is a hub airport, a connection to Orlando wouldn't be difficult to find. He flew to Atlanta, a connnection to Atlanta was impossible to find. He spent the rest of the night alone, sleeping on a bench in Atlanta airport.

Perversely he seemed to enjoy that little adventure and the slice of solitude it granted him. The legacy of tiredness it left him, however, kept him ragged for the rest of the tournament. On the training field at Seminole County that Friday he was barking like a drill sergeant. He would wander through the lobby of the hotel, distant and distracted, parking himself occasionally in front of the big screen at the bar to sample some of the action from another group. The football would draw him out and he would implore those around him to get a load of this "referee's decision just here". Then suddenly he would be up and off. Gone.

> *Over the years, the Irish job has given Jack Charlton an extra dimension.*

When it all ended, in the crashing, mistake-beaded defeat to the Dutch on Monday, 4 July, Jack seemed freed of a great weight. His players shed their tears and made their oaths and spoke of their regrets. Jack was philosophical. "I'm happy enough to leave it at that," he told a press conference in the moments following defeat. He was defiant and snappish and as disinclined as ever to pass the time of day with the media but there was no twist of bitterness. Defeat came at the end of struggle and then there was peace and life again.

Outside there was singing. These fans wouldn't be rolling on to Dallas to see the lads joust with the Brazilians. They would be going home to face debts and the other weights of reality. They were calling for their king. On the podium Jack mused about the nature of the defeat, about the mistakes and the sympathy he had for the perpetrators. The mind flashed back to a million Leeds games and every time the ball found the back of the Leeds net Jack would be compulsively remonstrating with somebody. There was always blame to be dished out after a goal. Here on this podium, though, he is shrugging his shoulders and seems about to give out a chorus of "Que Sera Sera". His temper isn't good but he looks for all the world like a man who has read and absorbed Kipling's words about triumph and defeat. Winning is still a pleasure, but as life fills out defeat isn't such a nightmare. For Leeds and England he had railed against defeat mightily. Now he wasn't so sure what had driven him.

Over the years, the Irish job has given Jack Charlton an extra dimension. He has played football for money since he was fifteen and life has held precious little else but that obsession with a game where winning matters more than anything. In Ireland he encountered a culture where participation was an innocent joy, where half a million people lined the grey streets to hail a gallant losing side. He isn't a deep man but the impression Ireland made ran deep. Somewhere he was unearthing old values and priorities lost since childhood.

Best's question is easily answered. Jack has had the bottle to compete and keep on competing for decades. Granted a vastly inferior talent to Best's he hasn't been afraid to confront himself and make the most of it. Bottle in the end is finding yourself and your limits and living life with that knowledge for company.

Those hours after the defeat in Orlando had an end-of-era feel to them. Ireland was passing Jack Charlton by in slow motion. The nation buoyed and encouraged by its own distorted view of itself was moving to a phase where winning was starting to matter more than just playing. Losing was beginning to hurt a little more. Celebration was called for still, but this dance had a more complex theme.

Jack, Big Jack, the man who unfolded this great world of wonder for us, was moving in the opposite direction. He was moving ever closer to fulfilment. Reluctantly in the wake of defeat he would go home. He noted the waning of Irish innocence, the altered nature of celebration, the dawning of a passionate hunger which he once knew in himself. The gratitude came to him in waves. He had opened this door for them. He has often said that he will leave the Irish job when the Irish people no longer want him. He will stay surely to

bring a new and blossoming team to England in 1996, where all the binds of being away from home will vanish. He will enjoy that. He knows now that the time won't come when the Irish people demand his resignation. The good times have left too strong a bond for that to happen. He will go because the Irish have lost something and he has gained something. The strands of the great narrative, football, Ireland and Jack will have been lost to each other. One day Ireland will return to the footballing backwaters. Defeat will be a harsh wind in our faces. The legend of the big Geordie will have grown still greater then.

By the end, you know, nobody really noticed that when speaking of Ireland, he used the word home.

Acting in the national interest. With Albert Reynolds at Dublin airport, July 1994.

Copyright © Weidenfeld and Nicolson Ltd

First published in Great Britain in 1994 by
George Weidenfeld and Nicolson Ltd
The Orion Publishing Group
Orion House
5 Upper St Martin's Lane
London WC2H 9EA

This edition produced for the Book People Ltd
Guardian House, Borough Road, Goldalming,
Surrey GU7 2EA

A catalogue record for this book is available from
the British Library.
ISBN 297 83466 5

Edited by Lucas Dietrich
Designed by Bradbury and Williams
Designer: Bob Burroughs
Litho origination by Pixel Colour Ltd, London
Printed and bound by Butler & Tanner Ltd,
Frome and London

PICTURE SOURCES
Allsport/Inpho/Billy Stickland: half-title, title,
4-5, 8-9, 9 (top and bottom), 10, 11, 12 (top and
bottom), 12-13, 14, 15, 16, 17 (top and bottom),
58-9, 60, 61, 62-3, 63, 64, 65, 66-7, 67, 69, 70-1,
71, 72-3, 74, 75, 76, 76-7, 80, 81, 82-3, 84, 84-5,
86, 88, 90-1, 92-3, 93, 94, 95, back endpapers
Allsport/Hulton Deutsch: 22, 27, 33, 34-5, 36-7,
38, 40, 41, 46-7, 48, 50-1, 54, 55
Allsport/Mirror Syndication International: front
endpapers, 24, 29, 30-1, 32, 39, 42, 43, 44, 44-5, 49
(left and right), 51, 52, 53, 56, 57
Allsport: 6-7, 68-9, 72, 89
All Action: front cover, 87
Michael Kirkup: 18-19, 20, 21, 23, 25, 28
Angling Times: 26

FRONT ENDPAPERS: Charlton tussling with Peter
Houseman of Chelsea in 1971.
TITLE PAGE: At Dublin airport, after World
Cup 1990.
BACK ENDPAPERS: Seminole County training cen-
ter. Jack talks to his boys.